The Last of the Old Cardigan Ghosts

The Last of the Old Cardigan Ghosts

Idris Mathias

Dolbadau Road Press

All rights reserved. No part of this book may be reproduced, stored in a retrieval system, or transmitted, in any form or by any means, electronic, mechanical, photocopying, recording or otherwise without permission from Dolbadau Road Press, P.O. Box 363, Basye, VA, 22810, USA. Email: DolbadauRoadPress@gmail.com

Back cover illustration by Idris Mathias

Copyright © 2015 Idris Mathias
ISBN-13: 978-1511502078
ISBN-10: 151150207X

About the Author

Idris Mathias was born in the Mwldan area of Cardigan, Wales, in 1924. During WWII, he joined the Royal Navy and went to sea. When the war was over, he returned to Cardigan to work as a postman. He has written two other books: *Last of the Mwldan* (Gomer, 1998), remembrances of his childhood in Mwldan; and *Ghostly Tales of Old Cilgerran* (Dolbadau Road Press, 2014), a collection of mystical tales of the nearby Pembrokeshire village. He and his wife of 65 years, Beryl Mathias (author of *A Time to Remember, 2014*), live in Cardigan; their five children and numerous grandchildren and great-grandchildren live nearby.

Contents

Rhagymadrodd / *Introduction* 1
Ysbryd Twm y Nos / *The Ghosts of Twm and Nos* 7
Morwen / *Morwen* 11
Pwll Sgrech / *The Screeching Pool* 16
Ystabl Cyracfa / *Stable Hauntings* 19
Will-pob-man / *Everywhere Will* 27
Dai Penwan / *Light-headed David* 29
Ci Tan y Cwm / *The Firedog of the Cwm* 31
Twm Cwlwm / *The Knot Man* 34
Yr Hen Derwen / *The Old Oak Tree* 36
Ladi Wen / *White Lady* 40
Dafydd Bach Swci / *Little Gentleman Dai* 44
Mochyn Du Bach / *Little Black Pig* 46
Ysgerbwd y Cei / *The Quay Skeletons* 49

Magi'r As / *Maggie the Bitch* 51
Meddyg Llaw Coch / *The Red-Handed Doctor* 57
Toili / *Ghost Funerals* 62
Cabden Cwrw / *Captain Beer* 65
Heol y Cei / *Quay Street* 72
Trafferwr / *The Troublemaker* 74
Dyn Tal y Feidr / *The Tall Man of the Ghostly Lane* 77
Swnau y Coffin / *Coffin Disturbances* 80
Mam Gwallgof / *Demented Mother* 82
Llety Bont Godi / *The Drawbridge Inn* 84
Fanny au Clocs Atsain /
  Fanny Clogs and Her Ghost Footsteps 88
Melinydd Llwchus / *The Dusty Miller* 90
Cabden y Moch / *Captain Pig* 92
Dawns y Dal/ *Dance of the Leaves* 94
Ysbryd y Treath / *Strand Ghost* 96
Gôl Bach / *Churchyard Singer* 98
Plentyn Diolwg / *The Deformed Bastard* 102
Steps-y-Mwg / *The Smoky Steps* 107
Adar Meirw y Mor / *Seabirds Signifying Death* 109
Wrach y Dwr / *Water Witch* 111
Rhith-y-Gof / *The Phantom Blacksmith* 115
Clocs y Bont / *Upside Down Clogs* 117
Coeden Ladi Wen / *The White Lady Tree of Pwllhai* 120
Ysgerbwyd Dan Dwr / *Underwater Skeletons* 122
Ysbrydion Canu / *Singing Ghosts* 125
Ysgerbwd Rhwyfwr / *Eel Pool Skeleton* 127

Cwn Bach y Tylwyth Teg / *Tiny Fairy Dogs* 130
Rhiw Rhaff-Dalwrn / *Ropeyard Hill Apparition* 133
Tŷ Tafarn y Cigydd / *Butcher's Arms* 135
Will Cot-iar Llygaid Coch/
  Will the Red-Eyed Moorhen 137
Magwyriad y Nos / *Night's Invisible Wall* 139
Dafi Twpsyn / *Daft Dafi* 141
Dai Ti Mewn, Dai Ti Mas / *Dai Inside Out* 145
Cwilt Wraig / *Quilt Widow* 150
Rhith-y-Ffynon / *Water Spirits of the Well* 157
Matri Bach / *Tiny Matri* 164
Dilys-y-Gwynt / *Dilys of the Wind* 166
Mor-Forwyn / *The Mermaid* 168
Tywod yn Canu / *The Singing Estuary Sand* 171
Hen Wraig Pentan / *Chimney Corner Hag* 174
Twm Ffagod / *Twm Faggots* 176
Cannwyll Corff / *Corpse Candle* 177
Llety Hyddwen / *White Hart Inn* 179
Dial y Morwr / *Sailor's Revenge* 183
Cor y Lon / *The Midgets of Ebens Lane* 186
Pwll Dafi / *Dafi's Pool* 189
Eyllyll y Ffynon / *Elf of the Well* 192
Y Diafol Coch Dawnsiwr a Ladi Wen /
  The Dancing Red Devil and the White Lady 195
Menyw Llwyd / *Lady in Grey* 199
Y Bedd Heb Farw / *The Grave That Refused to Die* 200
  Afterword 202

Rhagymadrodd
Introduction

Welsh ghost tales and a whirlwind of reminiscences are complex enough in themselves. My mind captures a somber cloud of misty-eyed emotions and memories. I imagine myself coasting above the old streets of Cardigan, West Wales, inside a transparent bubble. I can recall the inhabitants going about their daily business. I can see the cats and dogs, I can hear the shouts and screams.

I have been 'ghosting' back to my childhood, to a forgotten time when the neighborhood I grew up in, Mwldan, was an active community. From my bubble, I can see the Little People, the Tylwyth Teg, the fairy people, the Lilliputians.

Mwldan has long since been razed to the ground, but the days of 'Idi' (that's me) and 'Willy Blod' (that's my brother), the two sons of David John and Blodwen Mathias, remain in my mind. The forgotten memories come winging back and keep gunning me to write all I can recall, in a sublime effort to relive the forgotten place of my birth.

In those times I would peep out the window of my attic Shangri-La and watch the moon wane and toll in silence. Memories of those spell-bound evenings take me on a journey where I spend quiet hours trying to put invisible stitches in the fabric of my mind.

Some nights were still, very still, as the moonlight gave way to darkness. Then suddenly the bright moon would reappear in all its glory from behind the fleeting clouds.

We grew up in a ghostly atmosphere. We listened to the eerie and scary tales of the paranormal and of the people who had lived in this house before us. Were they reluctant to leave?

There was a slow, dignified pathos in our mamgu's, or grandmother's, voice. We called her Mam Mam Cei. She touched our hearts with her stories of a sorrowful and long-suffering life, her troubled thoughts of long ago. We felt the strange sadness that weighed heavily on her old shoulders.

Mam Mam Cei would become completely absorbed in her tales. My eyes would fix on the mystic light emanating from behind her. She would say, 'Look at the future backwards.' Whatever did she mean? Her words would mostly puzzle us.

Mwldan never pretended to be a grand place to live, but to me it was home sweet home. As children, we could ignore the poverty that was around and about. Our days passed untroubled, and our innocence provided us with simple joys, enchanting beyond measure. We thought young thoughts in an old world.

My first breath was taken in a dark and claustrophobic kitchen, where my journey on this earthly body began on the last day of 1924. We never thought we would be the home's last occupants. It was a friendly place, even though a plague of cockroaches lived behind the thick kitchen wallpaper.

The kitchen was our auditorium, where we would listen to local gossip and ghostly tales. The fireplace would blaze with firewood collected from the nearby beach, and it lit up our faces as we listened to weird tales. The firewood would spew bolts of burning embers at us. We thought that meant the ghosts were angry with us.

The kitchen was no safe place to be, with its sudden amber lightning strikes and the smell of smouldering cloth. The fireworks display would illuminate the dark kitchen until it seemed full of burning meteorites. The scene resembled the wonderful sunsets at Golwg-y-Mor, or Sea View.

These were magical moments, until the rough night winds shook and roared inside the chimney and powerful draughts that sounded like ocean waves tore under the front door and up into the loose wallpaper. There it vibrated and whistled and chased the cockroaches into their tunnels.

On winter evenings, Mam Mam Cei and our mam would come together, regardless of what the weather threw at them, to chat and pass the night away. There in the kitchen darkness, the ghosts listened with us as we sat transfixed by their extraordinary tales of the spirit world.

We would hear about frightful happenings and haunts, and crazy characters who did awful deeds, unseen of course. There were many generations of eerie, very eerie, goings-on. It was no wonder we rubbed shoulders with Cardigan ghosts.

The tales were very scary but they were our communal heritage. Mam Mam Cei would sit in a corner chair reserved for her. She was very special in our young lives. She had lively high spirits and seemed to us an angel of the night, with a gift for getting the kitchen atmosphere just right.

As we sat there, warmly wrapped in woollen blankets, she would speak quietly but loud enough for us to hear every word, in Welsh. She had a habit of bringing a tale to an abrupt stop, leaving us to puzzle out the ending. On her next visit, she would finish it.

Those nights were wonderful, as we heard the dreadful haunting of the ocean winds. The whistling noises grew and ghosts danced to its rhythm. We imagined skeletons jiggering on the tin roofs doing the Dance of Death. We would listen to stories about the apparitions who flew on the backs of bats and played with the witches on their flying broomsticks.

When we were toddlers and the days were fine, Mam Mam Cei would take us on slow guided tours, stopping here and there, and pointing out where ships that had been important to Cardigan town had once berthed. She also pointed out the dangers of getting too close to the quays, telling us to beware of them since she had seen too many children drown.

Mam Mam Cei seemed spiritually stirred by the incoming tides and tidal surges. She loved the Teifi River. Mam had all her gifts. They were a living reflection of each other in manners and in thinking. Both had excellent memories. To us, they were the 'Dons of the Mwldan Nights.'

Do Cardigan ghosts still exist in this fast-moving world, now that many of the buildings and their superstitious inhabitants are long gone? Or have they moved on? They had their moments here!

I seem to be the last person left to share these creepy tales with others, those stories that once upon a time scared the life out of me and my brother.

Idris Mathias
Mab y Mwldan
(Son of the Mwldan)
Cardigan, Wales
April 2015

Ysbryd Twm y Nos
The Ghosts of Twm and Nos

This is the sad and forgotten tale of Twm and Nos. Twm was a boy who dreamed of following his brothers in ocean-going and seeing the world. He constantly bothered his doting parents for a chance to go to sea. When he was ten years old, an uncle who was a sea captain brought his ship into the port in Cardigan.

The ship's next short journey was to Ireland. Twm's parents thought he could go with his uncle and be back home in a week or so. They hoped that if he became seasick, he would change his mind about a life at sea.

At the quayside, his mother kissed him as the ship was ready to leave. Twm then bent down to kiss and cuddle his little black dog, Nos, which means 'night' in Welsh. Nos was tethered to a rope.

He waved his parents farewell as the ship drifted away in the outgoing tide. In the meantime, Nos struggled with the rope and managed to break free. He chased after the ship, racing over the drawbridge and across Netpool and up the path to reach the promontory turn in the river, Rhipyn Coch. Wherever Twm went, Nos had to follow.

Then Nos swam out in the ship's wake. Here the water was rough, and as Nos struggled to reach the ship, Twm caught sight of him.

Without a second thought, Twm dived overboard to reach his lifelong pal. A sailor saw this and watched Twm swim toward Nos. There was nothing he could do as the ship sailed on.

Twm and Nos swam together toward the shore, but the racing current soon swept them to their doom. Their bodies were found the next day on the beach of Traill Bach below Old Castle Farm. Twm was embracing Nos.

This heartfelt tragedy upset young and old. Later they were buried together in a cemetery. There was a very large funeral, and a headstone was placed above them, inscribed 'Twm Nos'. On the bank away from the river, they lay in peace.

It was a terrible time for Twm's family. Deeply wounded at their loss, his mother pined herself away to an early grave. As her death neared, she lay in bed with a lone candle to light the bedroom. Alone and almost in a coma, a teary mist dimmed her eyes. It was then she saw Twm and Nos looking at her.

Twm was on her left side while Nos stood on her bed. Twm spoke, *'Mam, y fi sydd yma gyda Nos.'* ('Mam, I am here with Nos.')

Slowly, she did her best to reach a sitting position. But she collapsed back on the pillows. Through her sunken eyes she saw the two of them as usual, full of mischief, with Twm holding her hand as Nos wagged his tail and licked her face. There was a happy bond between them.

She reached out her arms in a most welcome embrace. Her face was wet with tears. With her eyes closed, she heard Twm's young voice: *'Mam, gwrando, ma fi a Nos yn hapus iawn a paid a becso am ni, mae rhaid I ti gwella cyflum iawn!'* ('Mam, listen, we are very happy where we are and don't worry about us, you must get well as quickly as you can, and we both love you very much, get well, little mother, get well!')

Twm cuddled up to her in a wonderful tight embrace and Nos licked the tears from her face and eyes. She fell fast asleep with a smile on her face, and in her arms lay Twm and Nos.

In the morning, the family saw a miracle. She had made a remarkable recovery, and in a few days she was walking about on weak legs. Later she asked to visit the grave, taking with her a bunch of flowers. While there, she felt something touch her leg. It was Twm and Nos, standing beside the headstone. Twm was smiling at her.

In her twilight stroll, their shadows walked beside her, and the silence spoke for her. She was content to know they were next to her. She lived to be very old. Twm and Nos never aged and were her guardian angels.

The heavy headstone eventually became embedded in a stone hedge that held up the bank. It became a curiosity among the townspeople, a site to visit to recall the tragic memory. But as the years rolled by, people began to forget it was there.

Sadly, the headstone fell victim to vandals, who with great effort threw it into the river, where it was lost. Some local people tried to recover it, to save a part of river history, but it was not to be.

The vandals were never caught—they never are!

Morwen

Morwen

A young Mwldan girl named Morwen was haunted by apparitions of three ghostly children of her own age. Other did not see them. She didn't know it then, but the apparitions were her guardians who secretly protected her from harm.

Always at her side were two boys and a girl, all with fair hair and soft green eyes. She did not see them all the time, only in moments of impending danger. She also could see them on any reflecting surface, as they watched over her constantly.

Strolling down Netpool she knew they were with her, one boy on each side, with the girl following. They appeared only when they needed to, in times of stress or trouble, to guide her away, to save her pain. She would talk back to them, and when people saw her talking to herself, they thought she was soft in the head.

She finally told her parents about the apparitions that followed her. Her reward for telling them was a good hurtful smack on the head to knock some sense into her. As the years went by, she suffered bewilderment and stress.

At last, she thought, enough was enough, and she played with the idea of ending her life. One fine day when the tide was in, she swam out to the middle of the river and let herself go to her doom by drowning. But as she went under, she felt a strong pull bringing her back to the surface.

She passed out, and strong invisible hands dragged her to the bank below Netpool. Waiting people pulled her to safety and helped her regain consciousness. The first things she saw were her invisible children looking both annoyed and concerned at her wet condition.

She couldn't drown or kill herself no matter how hard she tried. They prevented her. Then one day she no longer saw them, not even in shop windows. Her visions had gone but the apparitions were now in her thoughts, controlling her wild behaviour.

She grew older, fell in love, and had three beautiful fair-haired children with green eyes—identical to the children who had followed her around and saved her from getting hurt. She became their earthly mother. They had saved her so they could be born. Many times she wondered how the un-living apparitions managed to know that she was to become their mother, her living offspring.

She pondered and pondered without any reasonable answers. But nowhere in the entire area was there a happier family, part ghost, part human.

What other family secrets are beyond human understanding?

Although our grandmother—Mam Mam Cei— was as old as old can be, we worshipped the ground she walked on. She told tales as old as the hills. The women who came into our house for fireside chats had carefree hours to say what they liked without being ridiculed. They had the extraordinary ability to express themselves and tell tales never heard before.

Cold nights meant a get-together, and our kitchen was a background for ancient dramatics to inform and entertain. We would listen to dreams of countless expectations, of glowing possibilities, and of course confidential chats—even though little ears must not be within hearing range of what was said.

Some of the long evenings exhausted us, and we would sneak upstairs in the gloom, our faces bland and cherubic. We tucked ourselves into bed hearing their laughter below. They made us feel safe, and we could drift off knowing that all was well—except for the painful sucking fleas that feasted on our bodies.

Many nights my sleep was disturbed with nightmares, fluctuating from Twm and Nos to the haunted girl with the three apparitions. I feared peeping out from under the blankets, since I didn't need any of those ghosts sneaking in beside me. I had a nasty habit of reliving the tales while in deep sleep. I developed a fear of drowning that seemed real, and I struggled with terrifying feelings.

Later in the darkness, I would wake in alarm to frightful moans that filled the attic. My arms and legs thrashed around in my attempt to avoid drowning. I cocked my ears to listen, but I could have cut the silence with a knife. My breathing was irregular, coming in fast short pants.

The exhaustion was so strong that I would hold my breath for as long as possible. With a few heavy deep sighs, I fell back asleep. In the morning, I remembered all the nightmares, and the measles spots on my body were the damned flea bites.

Our young lives were surrounded by the paranormal. One day, as I lazed quietly on the grass looking up into its rich green branches, a few yards from the cemetery wall, I was able to hear my own heartbeat. Then it suddenly came to me that icy skeleton fingers could rise from under me and grab me!

I leapt to my feet while the other boys laughed at my efforts to get away. Further down Netpool I found a safe place to sit down above a lonely promontory. I looked down at the beach where parts of rotting ships had sunk in the mud. I could also see the Pant Cottages and the Teifi River, a weird place of legends and ghost tales.

We heard of an eerie tale of something that was seen downriver, a drifting heavy grey mist that covered Pwll Sgrech (the Screaming Pool) like a cloud about the riverside woods. It just hung there, motionless and threatening, silent and brooding, when suddenly out of it flew unusual white birds that circled the clear surface part of the river.

At top speed, they returned into the mist as quickly as they had appeared: they were the Premonitory Birds of Death!

They were known as 'Cacwn y Meirw' to the older inhabitants. To those who saw them, it became their time to worry, as they foretold imminent death to family or friends, doom and gloom.

Dear old Mam Mam Cei would say, 'There are idle moments when the mind goes blank. It drifts away on its own waves and gives the unthinking things beyond everyday eyes.'

Pwll Sgrech
The Screeching Pool

Pwll Sgrech could not be seen. In its place we saw a mountainous raging ocean tossing a vessel in distress, a stricken phantom ship. The waves blotted the whole river. She was sinking, torn flags and flaying and shattered rigging. Was she drifting back to her home port?

It was a terrible scene. The sailors had lashed themselves to what remained of the shattered wreck as the ocean played cat and mouse with their lives. This phantom scene blocked out everything, and those who watched couldn't escape the gruesome horror as it happened in some distant ocean.

People were mesmerized until suddenly the ship and storm vanished. It had all been a trick of the mind. The same thing happens on winter evenings, when in a static moment the mind becomes receptive to forces beyond its control, taking in unusual ghostly spirits.

Now we are the rising generation, in awe of the ancient tales. I recall difficult and sad evenings as a child in the Mwldan, when the older folks reflected on the loss of a relation in the war, at sea, or in the coal mines. There would be quiet interludes; their horizons were far away. Now it seems that we have come to take their places.

Once, off the quays, we were caught throwing stones into the high tide. Mam had seen us and called, 'Don't go near the river!' She was sitting with her mam looking down the river. I saw tears in Mam Mam's eyes and the infinite peace behind them. It seemed that bitter troubles were her lot on that lovely day on Anna Betsy quay.

For all the vexation of her spirit, she kept peace with herself and the changing world about her. It was one of those dreamy days in the warm sun. She seemed caught between two conflicting regrets and yearnings of what could have been. She looked at her daughter and said,

'Blod, mae pryd I codi'r angor,' or *'It's time to raise the anchor,'* meaning it was time to go home.

On quiet days, I was enthralled with the beauty of the vast sea and the calmness of the Teifi River. The soaring gulls and the crows, with their sharp calls, seemed to be trying to annoy each other. Children could run and fall on the lush green grasses of Netpool without getting hurt.

When people of importance walked along the road and raised their walking sticks, it meant we had to get off the road, as it belonged to them. They stared at us sullenly, as if we were freaks of nature. I felt hurt by their arrogant behaviour toward us; it gave me a guilt complex—had I done something wrong towards them? Perhaps they just thought we were flea carriers.

One day, at the crossroads above the stinking gasworks, there was a furious battle between two groups of boys. It was gang warfare, as they threw stones at one another. Then some men out for a walk ran after them with their walking sticks and the boys got trapped. The men thrashed their heads, until the boys got away and dashed down to the beach, full of hurt and tears.

At times, a young girl would sing while seated on the end part of the hill wall. Behind her stood the tall metal gas lamp overlooking the lower Mwldan. She was a picture of happiness. She would chat with Mam Ma Cei; they were related, the very old and the very young.

Ystabl Cyracfa
Stable Hauntings

The husband was in the back stables tending to the horses before retiring for the night. It was dark and stormy, and gale-force winds combined with heavy downpours. It was a troubled evening, and the horses were restless.

Two sisters sat before the kitchen fire in deep conversation. It was their usual routine before Christmas each year, a seasonal get-together. Their children were fast asleep in an upstairs room with a window that faced the church. The bedroom door was left ajar should the children cry.

The sisters were drinking tea out of coloured basins, content in their low talk, when all of a sudden the temperature dropped and a chill infiltrated the air around them. The coldness affected the very core of their beings, and they shivered before the fire.

They looked at each other forebodingly and lit more candles. Each with a candle, they searched around the ground floor and found nothing out of the usual. With woollen shawls around their shoulders, they took a quick look outside the front door and saw it was raining.

They had a sudden premonition that their children sleeping in the front bedroom were in some danger, so they took the stairs as quietly as they could. Their flickering candles sent horror shadows dancing along the walls, and the stairs groaned under their weight. They reached the landing. The bedroom door was still partly open. They took a few steps to the bedroom and peeped in.

They froze where they stood. Three apparitions resembling monks of old in their habits were in the room. One was at the top end of the children's bed and the other two were at the bottom end. They seemed to be enthralled, as they silently inspected the children, making hand signals referring to the bed.

The bedroom smelled of mouldy straw or ancient grass. The spell was broken when one of the children groaned and moved. The ghostly figures seemed alarmed and without haste turned away from the bed to make a line towards the right corner. As they did, the children's tomcat followed them as they disappeared through the solid wall!

Confused, the sisters looked out the window and saw it was snowing. They had another surprise when they looked down and saw tracks appearing in the snow made by invisible people walking towards the church grounds and the ancient priory. A blizzard was now raging over the Pont-y-Cleifion area of the lower town.

One sister went downstairs and opened the front door to find it raining, while the elder sister in the bedroom looked outside and saw snow blowing in a gale, a truly amazing sight. It was unbelievable. They changed places, and as soon as the other sister left the bedroom everything had changed back to rain, and the snow had gone.

They quickly moved the children to a back bedroom for fear that the ghosts would come back and snatch them.

They searched for the tomcat for days after without success. That evening was sealed in a veil of mystery. It was a Christmas they would never forget.

A year later, almost to the evening the tomcat had disappeared, the sisters were sitting before the raging fire when some strange and unsettling noises came from the bedroom. With flickering candles, they went upstairs to investigate.

Last year's phenomenon was back. The same shadowy figures appeared and disappeared, and the upstairs stank of rotting straw. They looked out the bedroom window and saw a snow storm raging. One sister went downstairs and opened the front door to see it raining.

The apparitions eventually made their way toward the corner, and as they went through the wall a very large snowball, like a comet, flew into the room and crashed open. It was their lost tomcat. He had been missing an entire year. He shook himself off and calmly walked down the stairs, leaving puddles of melting snow on the floorboards.

The blizzard disappeared and the tomcat licked itself before the fire. One of the sisters dried it with a towel and fed it. It laid back to enjoy the fire, home safely after a year away. The sisters wondered what tales it could tell after a year with the monks of the old priory, centuries ago.

To their surprise, sloppy footprints appeared in the room, as if the apparitions were back looking for the tomcat. They thought maybe some daft person could follow the monks through the wall and stay a year with them. They found someone to do it, who mixed with the monks and returned with a few strangers out of the past who talked in a funny way.

Then one of the sisters took a journey back through the wall to see what life was like there. The bedroom now became a place where time travel was possible. They could see strange children play with theirs, running about the stables. Thing got more and more curious, but the sisters just kept quiet, smiling.

What other wonders were out there? Those people had discovered a way back through the centuries. The Pont-y-Cleifion stables became a mausoleum to time travel.

Listening to ghostly conversations infected my thinking with sadness and fear. In the semi-darkness, the little kitchen window resembled a half-closed eye. The front door was left wide open and neighbours would calmly walk in. Some were more welcomed than others. They were admired and loved or disliked or pitied, but everyone had distinct folk tales from a bygone age.

When women came to visit, Willy and I had to go aloft to bed, as adult talk didn't interest us. The best gossip came after we left. As the saying goes, never reveal any secrets in front of children or drunks.

Wrapped in our blankets, we would creep silent as a mouse to reach the hole in our bedroom floor. Our backs were under the double bed our sisters slept in. It was our listening hole, and we could see who was in the kitchen and learn who was ill and who was dying. It was gloom and doom all evening, but we still listened.

One woman said she had seen a ghost and that it was following her around. Did she bring it into our house? Was it flying about in our attic? Were there more of them? Their horror forms played phantom tricks with my imagination as I fell sleep, with dreams of moths with wingspans of six feet fluttering about.

Then there was a sudden and sharp creak as the bed jerked and a tiny candle went out with a mighty explosion. My scalp was needled to the ceiling, and I was floating above the bed. The moths were dragging me out from under the blankets.

My arms were flaying about and my legs were kicking desperately. Willy nudged me to be still, but ghosts were ghosts, and I could see them rising out of the floorboards. Their icy bony fingers were cold on my face. The voices below in the kitchen continued to give me a vicious nightmare. I tried to keep the bad dream under control as I struggled underneath the blankets, and soon the ghosts disappeared. I fell into a deep slumber, oblivion at last.

I woke with the morning light streaming in through the window. I felt where the ghosts had stuck pins and needles in me, and then realised they were flea bites. It was no wonder: I would rush out of the house with our dog yapping happily at my feet. Was there a happier pair?

I would be asked, 'Why do you run out in such haste?' 'Out there I find independence and freedom, to do as I please, to think as I please, and to be far away from any adults!'

All lived lowly lives between hope and despair. They struggled to find enough food for their children. Through troubled years, they were the half-starved survivors of poverty and ill health. Talking to Mam, they found some solace.

One woman, with penetrating eyes, gave me the creeps. Her scary voice was that of a possessed person. We sat, unable to move as she spoke. We soon needed to escape her tales of horror and witchcraft. She seemed caught between the natural and unnatural worlds, a ghostly visitor with expressive emotions. Many a frightful night my brother and I slept sandwiched between two rough and bulky straw mattresses, squashed so as not give a ghost any room. How many times did we tell each other not to listen to her? She was a witch in her own right and practiced witchcraft in our house.

But we never learnt how to stop listening to this scraggy old woman, who looked too ill to walk, as if she had just risen from the grave.

Will-pob-man
Everywhere Will

Will was taking a walk late one evening and happened to meet an apparition. She was the most charming and lovely girl of his dreams. Had they met before? She wore a transparent gown. Almost touching him, she stared into his eyes and whispered with a light voice resembling the tinkle of bells.

Her words rang loudly in his ears: 'Nice to meet you "again," Will.' He could see the opposite hedge through her transparency and thought, 'Nice to meet you "again," Will'?

He was puzzled. He had never met such a beauty before. How did she know him?

The passing week was a revelation to him. He had found some lovely rapport, he was sure of that. Her loving eyes had penetrated his soul. His heart was spinning. He was deeply in love with her.

'Nice to meet you "again," Will.'

'Nice to see you, too, my sweetheart.' He was getting himself aroused.

He didn't realize it, but the years went by and he was getting older, yet she remained ever young. He knew he had fallen in love with a ghost.

His secret passion was to collect dead birds and bury them in the lane where they had first met, so that she could hear a springtime chorus through the dreary winter months.

This he did until his dying day. He died hearing his beloved songbirds singing loudly in his ears. Now, at long last, he was united with her through eternity.

Will-pob-man walked arm in arm with his ghostly sweetheart. He whistled with his ever-young birds and his ever-young sweetheart. Heaven was theirs.

Dai Penwan
Light-headed David

The gossip was about Dai Penwan, a very strange man who was given to conscious dreams and illusions of himself. Another man or several different men had invaded his body. He was a walking, talking confusion of personalities.

One dark evening on a cold street, as he made his way home, he was confronted by a ghost. He tried to bypass it, but the ghost blocked his way. Touching nose to nose, Dai saw a resemblance of himself in the ghost, but his mirror reflection was toying with him. With each able to enter the other, it confused him, and he wondered who he really was.

He was in a quandary. With eyes staring at each other and locked within each other, he was able to see backwards and forwards all at once. A few different minds were talking to each other, taunting the other or others.

A sudden shout almost made him jump out of himself. It was a passing drunk who needed to know the time. Dai, unable to answer, gave the man a kick.

Dai shouted to himself, 'Which one of you did that?' The drunk replied, 'There are only two of us on this street.'

Frightened of being left alone, Dai helped the drunk home. The drunk was curious as to who was who, and how many there were. When the drunk's wife appeared at the front door, she gave poor helpless Dai a hard slap across the face, forgetting her drunk husband.

Some days Dai was happy as a lark, but on other days he was weeping his troubled heart out, with his sad head resting on his wife's lap. On some days, he was the wisest of men, with a multi-brain of his other identities. When he died and was buried by his wife and family, it was a sad time for them—until they got home and saw Dai sitting comfortably, warming himself before the fire.

Ci Tan y Cwm
The Firedog of the Cwm

The Cwm outside the nearby village of St Dogmaels was a foreboding place even in daylight. It was damned worse in the hours of darkness. Older inhabitants would testify about the brooding silence and ghostly whispers that followed every step they took down the narrow lane. It was as quiet as silence can be, and it stalked every walker who dared go out in the darkness.

There would appear a floating flame, and even in a panic it was impossible to outrun it. Out of the flame appeared Citan, a large black hound with big fiery eyes. The local people shivered as he howled at their doors. One old couple was not scared of him, though, and they remained close friends over the years. They lived farther up the Cwm, and Citan made sure they got home safely, his fiery glow showing a clear pathway.

This couple's granddaughter had suffered since birth from an irritating rash. But a change came over her as Citan licked her all over. She was cured!

Once a desperate young mother carried her sick and dying infant son to visit her parents living farther down the Cwm. When the fiery hound suddenly appeared, the mother fell in a faint, dropping her baby on the grass. When she regained consciousness, she saw the hound breathing on the infant, guarding over it.

As she began creeping over to her child, the hound left. She lifted her baby and tried to run, but her weak legs refused to hurry. By the time she reached her parents' home, the baby was breathing easier and making happy grunts. To her surprise the child began to suckle her breasts. He made a remarkable recovery and lived to be one hundred years old.

The Cwm residents inscribed a large prehistoric standing stone with the words 'Carreg Ci Tan,' to show their appreciation to the Phantom Hound of Cwmdegwel.

Through the succeeding generations, those who could leap over the stone proved they were soon to become adults. The girls kissed it and put their ears to it, and it would tell them the names of their husbands-to-be. By rubbing their hands on it, they cured rashes and pimples and all sorts of conditions, warts and all.

Even the travelling gypsies knew of its curative powers, and they treated their animals as well. As the years rolled by, the stone was removed and dumped because it was too near the road, which had to be made wider for passing traffic. Local history was wiped out by the authority vandals. It was a most unfair treatment, and a cold shadow fell on Cwmdegwel.

Twm Cwlwm
The Knot Man

Twm Cwlwm possessed a remarkable memory. He was unable to read or write, but he could read the Bible forwards and backwards. He sang with the best of voices.

But his fame came with the knotted strings he wore around his neck. The various spaces between the knots were his Memory Knots, and only he could understand their meaning. They were his secret diary, and he could read them with his fingertips.

In his kitchen, he had rows of them gathering dust. On quiet evenings he would take some down and was able to remember things. He would laugh out loud at what they told him. As he grew older, the knotted strings grew larger.

When he died, his ignorant relatives burnt them.

We grew up listening to Mam and Mam Mam Cei telling their folktales and ghost stories. Their courteous goodnights echoed up to our attic room. 'Time to lift the anchor, Blod!' And away they went, with Mam escorting her mam to her house just around the corner.

Willy put the candle piece out, and our friends the moths were safe from being burnt. Then they had to be careful of the spiders' webs. It took us time to get to sleep, with the vampire fleas sucking their fill with our blood. The moths were a tasty meal to the bats, which came circling about, catching them before finding their way in and out by echo-location. Our attic was a sea of night-time activity of insect death and dying.

These somber reflections are no different to other parts of Wales during the poverty years. And now Mwldan is no more, having been totally obliterated and fallen into oblivion.

Yr Hen Derwen
The Old Oak Tree

Martha Gwen was an elderly woman. She once told us a tale she had heard about a man who disregarded the strong advice given to him to leave the Old Oak tree alone and not damage it. But he told himself that the warnings were just idle gossip, and he took an axe and chopped off a branch. On the ground, the branch twisted about in pain.

The Old Oak shook violently, and from somewhere came loud painful yells. Frightened onlookers took to their homes before they got cursed.

The man built a fire and threw the branch on it. As the flames engulfed it, a demonic and loud whistling noise hurt the ears of those who heard it.

The branch burnt into charcoal, and later the charred remains of a little black human skeleton rose and disappeared. For days after, the man was haunted by something unseen. It strangled him as he tried to sleep and kept him awake until he reached the point of madness. He screamed in night horrors and had terrifying nightmares. What was this unknown force?

The uncanny force made him build a large bonfire, and he threw himself on top of it. As he burnt, he let out loud screams. As the flames built up around him, his charred charcoal remains appeared as a black skeleton.

He had been warned not to injure the Old Oak, and his punishment was that he committed suicide—a lesson to any other would-be transgressors!

There was always a chill in the air when we entered our home. Mam would go get a log for the fire, to cheer the dark interior. We didn't have much in the way of worldly goods. There was no money to put nourishing food on the table. We were dependent on the breadline—it was bread with this, that, or the other; it was our basic daily requirement. We were no different from any other family there. But we had something more precious than gold—we had each other.

Our vaulted kitchen wall had patterns, and the flames soon had the devil himself appearing on the walls and dancing and leaping in all directions. He, too, seemed to show his appreciation to have us all home; he had been lonely without us.

Our caring mam would chat with us before the fire. It was not idle chatter, as she could be very serious in her calm, dignified manner. Her smiles made us feel good and put joy in our hearts. I wouldn't have changed our togetherness for the world. We might have been dismayed with our rudderless existence, but we had a happy home, and a fascination with haunting tales.

We sat around the table to have bread and jam and cups of tea, laughing and grateful to have the best mother in the world. She was easy in discipline unless we behaved badly.

We children had a cosy corner all to ourselves near the raging fire. There I imagined I saw a wild horse taking an upward flight with the flames and disappearing into the freedom of space. There was no end to my imagination.

Mam Mam Cei would appear when she needed company, and soon there would be much humour in our conversation.

Our eyes got accustomed to the bright crimson colours and the glow of our ocean sunset fire. The logs came from the incoming tides.

One evening we were entombed inside our dark kitchen listening to the crackling flames when we heard the front door open. It was Mam Mam Cei, so Willy, myself, and our sisters Mona and Connie shifted over to make room for her. While having her cup of tea sitting next to the fire, she told us the tale of Ladi Wen (White Lady) who lived in the tall trees.

Ladi Wen
White Lady

The mystical Ladi Wen came into being in the mists of long ago, when the Earth was very young and endless forests stretched from coast to coast. Hidden in their roots lived the devil without light, without end. Beneath the Mwldan moon, branches waved in the wild wind like ocean waves, and evolving spirits, witches, wizards, and white ladies cast and wove their ancient spells.

One special oak had not been born on its dedicated spot. It had been held back by the Druid gods. It spoke of a time within time when no one dared to look in pools of water to see the unseen, lest they suffer the evil consequences: to walk about without their second self, a half soul treading the Earth, a half human being.

Below in the underworld, Annwn, a dancing devil, and his kindred thrived in the subterranean abysses. But this dancing devil, when on the hill above Lower Mwldan, was a splendid fellow rampaging in 'jigs' with those who were once enemies but were now night-time companions to dance on the long winter nights. Their wild pranks entertained the woodland animals, who also danced.

From Ladi Wen's womb an acorn fell to reach its predestined spot. Through its infancy the tree was well guarded by large and boisterous crows with rows of razor-sharp incisors. They had the most savage tempers. As the tree grew in strength, the crows vanished, and it became a towering home for generations of wild animals and insects.

If any part of the tree was used in ship building, that ship was cursed to flounder on her first voyage and all hands would drown. Some men dared to take sections to make furniture, but the furniture turned out to be their coffins within a year of the committed offense.

The tree was protected by threefold spirits: Ladi Wen, the Devil, and an unseen crow. These haunting guardians gave the inhabitants the creeps, to keep them from touching the Divine Oak. It was to be the Tree of Doom for many.

'They who dare hath but twelve months to live!'

In bed one night, while trying to sleep, from outside we heard a strange voice with an upper-class English accent, like a private-school-educated chappie. He was a loud-mouthed bully bred to lead and take advantage of any maiden willing to listen to his titled hog-gobbing twang. He was unacquainted with the area, and here for one specific reason: Sex!

A woman's voice was heard, describing his silly chatter, 'Ma fe siarad fel moch Parc-y-Felin!' 'He talks like the pigs of Parc-y-Felin!'

Disturbing the night with his hoggish voice, he was out on our slate roof doing what he came there for, when someone threw a large length of dog excrement onto the roof. It tumbled towards him and landed near his feet. He shined his torch light on it and remarked, 'Goodness me, that bat's got a large anus.'

A few days later he was in a silly argument with some local lads who loved taking the 'piss' out of him. He thought he was a person of some importance and walked about like a cockerel in a fine tweed suit. He was ready to thrash all the lads, not one by one but all six together. But they were having nothing of his high and mighty speech.

They laughed at him for not being able to take a joke. Down Ebens Lane came a toffee-nosed woman looking for her husband. She saw the local lads having a jolly fun with a stranger and said, 'John, what on earth are you doing in these slums? You should be ashamed of yourself keeping company with such ruffians!'

A loud voice then said, 'My lord, tell the lady where you were two nights ago.' Red-faced, the man quickly escorted his wife back to High Street. They were never seen again. But he had his 'oats' on our slates, at a price.

The dark recess behind our roof was secretly called 'Clifach.' It was a journey's end for sexual encounters. That is, until a drunk wanted a piss and couldn't care who he pissed over. A fight would start and we would hear their foul words echo through the night.

The lovers' intoxicated chatter revealed the mysteries of sex life in the raw. We would hear the half-cocked lover talking to his penis, 'Rise, you old devil, stand and wait. My dear woman, I'll be ready in a moment!' But her patience would give way. 'You hound of heaven [a preacher], hurry up or we'll be late for morning service.'

The past sends ghostly messages to us in the form of old beliefs and superstitions: phantom funerals, phantom people, trees that can change shape; divine bees, cats, birds, mice, rats, corpse candles, and running shadows along the Mwldan.

Dafydd Bach Swci
Little Gentleman Dai

A man named Dai had a deep fascination for Ladi Wen, the White Lady that ghosted the streets. She greatly affected his life. From one night to the next, he saw fleeting glimpses of her. It seems that many years ago he had met her and had brief chats with her.

Local girls had a habit of teasing him. The White Lady had become the only love of his life. While waiting under an oak tree for her one night, down floated a flimsy gown. He carefully collected it—she had dropped it for him. Although he couldn't see her, he threw endless kisses up to where she was.

The slow endless years went by and his love for her never daunted. Poor Dai aged, and when he eventually died, they clothed him in his Ladi Wen gown. In the years following his death, many people swore they had seen Gentleman Dai being nursed in the fold of her arms, happy and content, and suckling her breasts like a baby.

Suckling Dai was in his ghostly utopia.

Mochyn Du Bach
Little Black Pig

The elderly parents had an only son who went to sea. With the money he had saved, he bought them a few piglets. Among them was a runt, a tiny black piglet that became their pet. Each time the son came home, the little pig followed him about like a dog.

But their friendship was not to last. The son died on a sea voyage, and his beloved parents cared for the pig as if it were their son. It was his gift of living, a faithful animal and most intelligent. It lived in the cottage with them and became the joy of their lives.

But the couple had jealous and offensive neighbours who constantly upset their lives. If that was not enough, the neighbours decided to steal the only worthwhile thing the couple had in their old age — their pig. The neighbours planned to kill it and make a feast of it.

One evening, while the pig was snorting about outside, it began squealing. The noise brought the couple out of their cottage in alarm, but being old and infirm they couldn't rescue their pet. The neighbors had hung him up and took out a sharp knife to slit its throat.

The couple had their arms around each other when they heard a voice come out loud and clear, 'Mam, Tad!' 'Mam, Dad!'

It was their son's voice pleading. The shock was too much for the wife, and she dropped dead. The husband tried to help her, but he too dropped dead.

The dreadful neighbours butchered the pig and set about making a meal of it, when all at once a fearsome apparition swept across above them. But laughing and joking, they went ahead and ate the ill-gotten black pig.

It was the last meal they would enjoy. The meat tasted bad; something was wrong with it. For days they suffered terrible stomach pains. The sickness resulted in a lingering and painful death for their wicked zeal. The little black pig took its revenge.

And the apparitions of the son and the parents stood on the bank watching, their revenge complete.

Ysgerbwd y Cei
The Quay Skeletons

The quay skeletons were a bizarre sight. People passing the quay entrance looked the other way so as not to see them. The creepy apparitions gave them the shivers.

When the dark clouds moved away and the moonlight shone, it revealed the Teifi wharf's curious pair: a husband and wife walking on each side of their donkey skeleton—a gruesome threesome.

Their bony heads would make jerky movements as they searched around and looked at each other as if in a deep conversation. They seemed to be looking for something or someone they couldn't find.

Their erratic jerking gave those who saw the skeletons sleepless nights. Others thought that maybe some treasure was hidden in the walls, and in daylight searched them, without success. The impossibility of finding something that the skeletons couldn't didn't deter them from looking.

Standing at the quayside with bony arms outstretched, the couple watched the full tide come in and hoped that the ship that went down with their son would reappear, or that a lost child drowned in the river would rise out.

Hereabout strange influences operated, and Mwldan was awake to them.

Magi'r Ast
Maggie the Bitch

A nasty-tempered hag lived in Feidrfair in St Mary's Lane. The nickname of Maggie the Bitch was given to her because of the many dogs she kept inside her home. She was brutal to them, kicking them and shouting endlessly, to the dismay of her neighbours.

The poor dogs barked and howled in their need to get out and about, mostly out of hunger. Any pups born were quickly devoured by other dogs. Maggie would roll in the dust fighting her distressed neighbours; she was one of those real rough and tough guys.

She had made many enemies, so her death was a relief to everyone. One night her house burned down, the blaze taking it to the foundations. There had been no escape for many of the dogs.

In the following years her ghost was seen struggling, carrying a dog by the scruff of its neck in one and a lighted candle in the other.

There is no escape from one's evil misconduct. The Devil took them all to their burning deaths, in the fires of Hell.

In my dad's riverside tale of the hound of the coracle walks in Cilgerran Gorge, he told how the dog would 'sniff' the ground while trotting along to Pwll-y-Pysgod (Fish Pool). The slick black hound would follow the fishermen below Forest Farm, and no one was sure where it would turn up next.

Was it leading the fearsome Cwn Annwn, or Devil Dogs of the Underworld, as they raced across the wet bog land, with the fires of Hell coming out of their wide mouths, chasing after some unseen prey? Some older fishermen remember the hound in their younger days, when it was ageless, forever young.

Illogical and irrational fears cunningly create ghostly illusions in the brain. These ancient riverside haunts, these otherworld entities, are the phantom wonders of the Teifi Gorge.

A lone white bull with very long horns roamed those woods. He was a rangy beast with the sudden speed of a greyhound. He would blur through the trees, giving the impression there was more than one of him. White ghostly forms were manifold there, especially wild horses that would swim across the river at Cwm-du, or the Dark Hollow.

One stallion made a powerful impact as he stood in the woods of Forest Farm and looked down towards Cwm-du, as if to challenge all. Where did these wonderful appa-

ritions originate? Were they following the ancient tracks of a bygone age, when white bears, boars, and wolves were seen in large numbers?

It was a golden age of story-telling, and we loved listening to the beautifully crafted tales of the unknown, of myth and magic.

My father was a good woodcarver and would spend many a happy hour sitting near the fireside chipping away as he chatted to me and Willy. The chips would pile up on his boots, and every so often he would throw handfuls into the fire. The pyrotechnics fascinated us.

With his sharp blade, models came to life. They were displayed on the mantelpiece. He spent joyful times with us, and he was in his element chipping away in a pensive mood. He was never loud or outspoken and had a quiet charm to his voice. He loved our togetherness, and he used his model-making to tell us weird tales.

His blade was his nib or handpen to his inner thoughts. The more chipping, the more models he created and the more tales of the riverside we heard—until a knock and a shout came to the front door. The blade would close, the chips would be thrown on the fire, and our evening would end as the women came in.

His half-finished models and half-finished thoughts had to wait until the next time, when he could finish his tales. To us they were the blessed evenings together as the wild weather rattled the tin roofs.

One of his riverside stories was about a large salmon. Some fishermen heard a tremendous splashing echoing along the river, followed by other crash-splashes, shattering the silence. They were puzzled and went to investigate. Strange, they thought, If a man was drowning, wouldn't he yell?

Then they saw a heavy swirling, and to their surprise a large and playful salmon appeared. It shone in the moonlight with the lustre of gold. Swimming in vigorous increasing circles, it made a whirlpool about two feet in diameter. The fishermen tried to net it, but it was like trying to catch the wind with one's fingers.

They couldn't net the illusive golden salmon. It was a formless, watery apparition. But it left a whirlpool in its wake, raising its head before going under. It was an elegant and magnificent King of Fishes, and it escaped the clutches of man.

Dad took me and Willy along with him to fish in the Piliau River. He was never in any great hurry to catch anything or go anywhere. Sitting on the bank, resting in the warm sun, he would recite his weird and wonderful riverside tales from his younger days. He was born in the coracle fishing village of Cilgerran, North Pembrokeshire, and possessed a remarkable memory. He knew enough English to get by. His parents were well-versed in the myths, legends, and wild beasts that lurked in the marshes.

He was a reserved and quiet father, and he had the charm and wisdom of a fairy being. To him, life outdoors was an enchanted fairyland.

His fireside and riverside and marsh tales came from his heart, and I have done my best to remember them as he told them to me. To us, the tales came alive with giants and fairies, with ghosts behind every tree. The marsh itself was haunted, and no one dared spend the night alone there. There were strange whisperings by lost souls.

A dark tunnel was made by old and tall trees binding on each side of the lane. In the darker shadows of the extending branches, many a ghost lurked like figurines. Rows of wild cats with red fiery eyes used the darkness to their advantage. They made any traveller's hair stand on end like the bristles of a hedgehog.

Below the trees, the overgrown brambles and giant ferns tangled, making any track impossible. Sightings were made of flying steeds with long white flowing manes waving backwards. They flew skyward, and on their backs were a fairy boy and girl with shoulder-length fair hair and green-blue eyes.

Spectral gold and white salmon leapt on the silvery river and reached the tallest tree top, then splashed back. They would sing in the sweetest voices, in Welsh of course. To the uninitiated, they had the power to understand the inner secrets of Nature.

Meddyg Llaw Coch
The Red-Handed Doctor

Sitting by the Teifi riverside, a young boy watched his father and uncle trawling in the coracles, when suddenly the men caught a very large salmon. They threw it on to the bank where the boy stood.

The boy watched it twitching. It looked at the boy, and there was an instant understanding between the two, even though no words were spoken.

The helpless salmon, through thought, asked the boy to help him back into the river, saying that in exchange for his life he would give the boy great powers to heal the sick.

The boy helped the salmon back into the river. It recovered and returned saying, 'You will be amply rewarded, wait and see, little boy.'

It slid back under the river and wasn't seen again. When the father noticed his salmon was missing, the boy had the thrashing of his young life.

Some weeks later, the colour of red spread from the boy's fingers to his elbows. His parents tried all sorts of quack remedies to remove it, but it remained redder than ever. Some time later, the boy's mother went seriously ill and was not expected to live the day and night out.

In turn, all the family, from the eldest to the youngest, took their final farewell to their mother. The boy came last. Before anyone could stop him, he was on her bed with his red hands firmly around her neck. They couldn't remove him from her, so they decided to leave him where he was, as his weakened mother requested.

Together they slept through the night. As the morning light came through the window, the mother sat up in bed while her son slept on. She asked for something to eat and drink. The brightness of the boy's hands had cooled to pink. Within a week she was back on her feet. The father suspected that his son's red hands had something to do with her cure.

Later, a young girl was extremely ill. Her parents begged for the boy to come to visit her. As the two children held hands, the parents could see the amazing change in their daughter's condition. Within a week she was out playing with her friends as if she had never been ill. It was a miracle.

Ill people in the village were made well again by the laying of his red hands on them. He became known throughout the area as Meddyg Llaw Coch, the Red-Handed Doctor. He never asked for any reward for his cures, and the village became a mecca for healing.

One day when he was grown and had a family, he was playing with his son near the riverside. He noticed strange ripples turn into large spins (to attract him), and then it saw him. The man and the salmon saw each other, and there was an instant rapport between them that had not changed over the passing years. The man was not able to believe his eyes. Here was the wonderful salmon that had given him the power to heal. Through their thoughts, the two wished each other health and happiness. After that, the salmon was never seen again.

The famed Red-Handed Doctor had been blessed by the Sea Goddess or the Mystic Salmon.

Their secrets are housed in the depths of Pwll-du, or Black Pool, and contain the ancient knowledge of older gods.

Willy and I listened to dad's voice as if we were travelling through time and space, into our dream-world, a place beyond imagination, a place of riddles. Yet isn't the past a dream to look back upon?

The demon whirlwind howled down the chimney and tore over the roof. Then it went quiet, an eerie silence as if a giant was holding his breath. Then it returned in a vile temper, letting out the shrieks of a woman molested by the Devil.

From the fireplace in our dark and claustrophobic kitchen, our Ghost Chamber, the stressed flames would try to reach out and burn us. The sparks were like shooting stars, shot out by the enraged and windy night. The chimney's breathing was akin to a blacksmith's bellow. The ferocity of a troubled night combined with those eerie tales and made me feel like I was like a ship in a gale, being tossed about.

The hurricane draughts made hissing and raging noises as they raced under the front door, sending bright sparks whizzing around and into dark corners. Was it the dancing devil, like a crazed ballerina, that made our dogs find comfort and safety in our laps, and eventually under my sister Mona's blanket?

Even when in company I felt alone inside. I gazed out of my green eyes, fixated on the tormented flames that beckoned me into them. Such was their demonic attraction that the cockroaches were lifted off the kitchen floor as if they had wings. Their tunnels under the wallpaper became wind tunnels, yet I never once heard them screaming.

To my real sorrow and loss, my only brother died a young man and is not here to assist me with my memories. He is now a silent partner in reflecting back to when Mam Mam Cei and Mam sat before the fire with tales of the Citan (Fire Dog) of Cwmdegwel, the cwm (hollow) outside the village of St Dogmaels, where she was born.

Toili

Ghost Funerals

The Toili, or spectral funerals, gave people who saw them the scariest experiences of their lives. They would appear in a most ghostly horror, and no matter how fast one would run, the funeral would still be at one's heels. Its slow progress was best watched from a great distance.

Should someone get caught in with the spectral mourners, there would be no escape; he would be forced to follow to the cemetery gates. If the gates were closed, he could not go through them and escape. If they were open, he would be taken to the grave and made to partake in the funeral service.

A lone woman on her way home in the dark along the Upper Mwldan happened to see a Toili coming down the hill. She had time to race across the bridge, but the Toili was almost upon her. She raced to the nearest house, which was the coach-builder's home, and knocked frantically at the door.

Her screams and fears knew no bounds. Confused, she fisted at the locked door and kicked at it. She shouted 'Let me in! It's me—it's me! They are coming to get me, for God's sake, let me in!'

An irate voice from behind the door calmly answered, 'I'm having a bath, wait until I get dressed.'

Falling on her knees, she was terrified; she hid her face in her hands and felt the chill of death. She took peeps through her fingers and saw the spectre horses, the hearse, and the ghostly procession. The women were wearing long black dresses and the men were in their frock coats and chimney pipe hats. She was too numb to remember all she saw. And who was in the coffin?

The Toili passed within a few feet of her. Maybe they didn't see her. As soon as they passed, she took a quick peep. There was no one about, so she raced blindly home towards the Bath House cottages where she lived. But her lingering thoughts of being led to the cemetery were too much for her, and she fainted outside her front door.

Toili fears were real enough. The spectral extra-dimensional spirits that appeared from the phantom mists had a blistering effect on people's mental states. They were ridiculed by those who had not seen them.

But if those same people were out walking in the dark and heard echoing footsteps following them, they ran hell-bent to get indoors.

On Netpool, there was a town park where all the children played happily in the sun. I was always interested in hearing what the old people there had to say, and this was probably the only place they would open up. We were their companions for a few hours. At the same time, we wanted to climb the trees with the other children. We never had a fear to listen to what others had to say, only amusement.

The loneliness of the area's leafy lanes was mine to relish, especially on bright sunny days. Birds in song would shatter the silence, and every moment was an adventure. As the woods got darker the deeper I went; they were full of unsettling mystery. It was like reading in the dark while resting in bed. Was there a better invention than a lit candle?

Cabden Cwrw
Captain Beer

The popular barber's shop situated on High Street was a 'talking shop' to all the gossip floating about, mostly full of malice. The corner end led down into College Row and the Mwldan area, and it had a fearsome reputation among the poor inhabitants. The owner was the pirate Cabden Cwrw, or Captain Beer, who had never been to sea. He was also called Cabden Torri Gwddwg, or Cut-throat Captain.

The locals had other devious names for the place, like Ghost House and Laddy (Slaughter

House), because hair-cutting and shaving often resulted in near-death misses to poor Mwldan residents who dared sit in the barber chair for a 'buckshee' shave by the apprentices, who had learned hair cutting and shaving with old, blunt razors in the backroom when Captain Cwrw was out—he was on duty on the bridge of the Ship Inn, filling up his gut! The apprentices would quickly shove their victims out the back door, their faces mummified with quick-drying paper to stop the bleeding.

Arthur was one of the local residents, a living zombie, and everyone knew what a stupid bonehead he was. One day, Arthur was walking down College Row opposite the barber shop. He was an easy target to the apprentice, who shouted him to come in. In went Arthur and sat down in the backroom chair. The young apprentice lathered him, and the shaky old razor cut and nipped him, and bits of papers blocked the blood seeping out of his face and neck.

The drunken captain returned and found Arthur demanding a pint of beer. Asking for a pint of beer was like asking for the crown jewels, the nectar of the gods. The captain raged, 'You have had a free haircut and shave, so why a pint of beer'?

'I need to find out if my neck is leaking!'

'Arthur, you go home and take this paper bag of barking dogs [meaning fleas] with you, and don't throw them in the river. The poor insects will be seasick. Drop them in the roadway and they will get out and follow you home. We don't need to see them return to this shop.'

Arthur sneaked out the shop by the back entrance, but before he left he asked the bulgy, red-eyed captain, 'How many days have I to live?'

The front room had two elegant barber's chairs where men were being shaved, while other customers sat in comfort around the room, which was a fine, pleasant place. In the backroom was a single spare chair and a bunk bed, where Captain Cwrw could recover from his drunken self. Sometimes he would plonk his paralytic self into the spare chair and snore loudly.

From time to time, he would jest with his apprentices, saying that one of them could cut his hair and shave his face. One quiet evening, as the drunken Captain Cwrw slumped in the spare chair, one of the daring apprentices took advantage of the situation and set about cutting off the captain's beard, giving him a clean shave (with a new razor). Then off came his hair, leaving a short back and sides, until he looked like a different person. The other apprentices laughed at him, and off they left him to his woes.

The captain woke up in a terrible rage—hangover and anger all in one. He slashed a cutthroat about like a cutlass. If he had caught just one apprentice, he would have chopped off his head. But his troubles had just begun. His wife refused him entry into his own home—she did not recognize the crazy stranger kicking at her front door. Even people walking the streets did not know this stranger walking and swearing in their midst.

His world seemed at an end. No one recognized the crazed man who strolled into the Ship Inn for a drink; customers refused to chat with a babbling baboon. In his rising anger, he became violent and kicked chairs about. He was booted out, no booze for him, and his pride took a bashing.

With wild and wide-open eyes, he returned to his shop. His apprentices were nowhere to be seen; they had hidden in the loft above the shop and were watching his every move through the floor spaces.

An elderly lady was sitting in a chair, waiting to confront him. But he quickly had a cloth around her neck and began lathering her, thinking she was a customer ready for a shave. She leapt out of the chair and kicked him in the shin. She cried, 'How dare you cut my son's face and neck! He has lost his voice and walks around with a brown paper bag over his head, with peepholes to see. What have you done to him?'

'Tell him to take a swim in the outgoing tide and around Cardigan Island and play with the seals, and to come back in on the incoming tide. That will cure him of his ills.'

'But what if he cannot swim that far?'

'You tell him it would do him a world of good to walk on the seabed and sing the song, "There's a devil in the cask of beer—so they say." When he comes home after his underwater stroll, Owen the Undertaker, with his fine hearse and fine horses, will take him for a ride. Afterwards, walk the lane ahead of the Toili and you will see your proud blockhead son lead the Toili along the Mwldan to carry people away!'

She shouted, 'You swine, you and that foul undertaker are in cahoots to share the booty. You supply the slaughtered carcasses and he supplies the cheap cardboard coffins painted to resemble expensive wood. Secretly you share the money, secretly made. You are the High Street cut-throat ghouls that shave ghosts. I have yet to see Cardigan ghosts with whiskers!'

She continued, 'Your barber shop is a ghost parlour torture chamber, and your victims reside on your roof. They never age.'

Meanwhile, Lisa Esgidiau (Lisa Big Boots), a small woman wearing men's heavy work boots that echoed behind her (her big mouth could be heard blocks away), stood out on the street opposite the barber shop and saw, with her second sight, the clean-shaven ghosts congregate on the roof.

Her vivid imagination brought people to gather around her as she pointed to a ghost face on the roof, claiming it was her departed relation. Others in the crowd claimed they saw departed relations.

'That's my Dai,' said one, and soon others saw their departed Fred, Gwen, Moira, Gwyn, Sam, Melys, and many others. Lisa's mouth hysteria edged the crowd on to see other things as well, as they called loudly to their ghostly relations. Her imagination stirred others to see things that didn't exist. They cried tears of joy to see their beloved ones again, to see the clean-shaved ghost faces that hadn't aged.

But soon their tears of joy turned bitter as they accused their departed, while alive, of being downright scoundrels, thieves, and untrustworthy cads. Even worse accusations echoed in the candle-lit night. Any stone found on the road was thrown at the roof-top ghosts, and the ghosts (it seemed) threw any loose slates onto the heads in the crowd, setting off a pandemonium of other evil spirits.

Above the melee, bats flew in circles, singing for the first time ever, and unseen owls screeched disapprovingly at the goings-on below. The stamping of feet, and Lisa's heavy boots, caused the road to shake like a mini earthquake.

Lisa Boots, by shouting verbal venom toward the roof-top ghosts, had done the impossible—she put the dead and the living in open confrontation. She was intoxicated by the night's events. A sudden gust of wind blew the candles out, and in a panic people raced home in the dark, falling in a tangle over each other.

There would be no sleep for them tonight. Noisy tomcats fought on tin roofs and dogs barked constantly. Doors were quickly bolted to stop the damned ghosts coming to get them. Lisa, in a foul mood, strolled along High Street and kicked at her right-handed shop doors, termed Wac y Mwniod, or Monkey Parade, after the wealthier inhabitants who loved showing off their elegant dresses.

People were awakened by Lisa's high-pitched screaming and thought it was some wild animal on the loose. Some opened their windows wide to throw excrement onto the street. The unfortunate people of Ebens Lane heard heavy boots shake their doors and windows, as Lisa Esgidiau made her roundabout way home. She had made more than enough mischief in one night of pure hell.

Heol y Cei
Quay Street

A seafaring family had a lovely young daughter who was but nine years old when she suddenly died. The effect on her doting parents was devastating. But she had known that one day soon her life would end, and she kept telling them that she would return and let them know how she was doing in Heaven.

In their kitchen, a sad and strange atmosphere surrounded them.

A few months after the girl's death, the distraught mother was preparing food for her family. To her alarm, she looked about her—something was tugging at her dress. There was no one there. She thought it must have one of her daughters playing tricks.

Later, her husband sitting before the fire had a shock to feel something drag at his trousers. He leapt to his feet to search around. His face showed alarm as he shouted, 'What's going on?'

The mother had other occasions when her clothes were dragged. Hardly daring to breathe, she sat across from her husband, and as they looked at each other the same thought came to them: Was it their departed daughter trying to make contact with them?

The mother asked, 'Is that you, Megan?'

There were more pulls on her skirt in answer to their questions, and eventually through time they came to understand that all was well with Megan. They felt proud in being able to talk with her. Although she was not with them, she was at home!

Trafferwr

The Troublemaker

On the cold, dark battlement steps of the church tower, an aggressive apparition tried to do the impossible: to launch himself off to reach Heaven. But he failed and crashed back onto the ground.

To fully understand his crazy behaviour, we must go back to the time when the town of Cardigan was terrorized by this vicious individual and his family. He was a nasty town troublemaker, a painful thorn to the community. He was an evil-doer, a devil-incarnate who was hell-bent on physical violence to injure others. There was no one safe from his criminal ways.

This bully once badly injured a young sailor who was having a quiet pint while his ship unloaded on the quay. When the sailor returned home to Norway, he explained to his family what had happened to him. Taking his place on the next voyage was his eldest brother.

He was there on the quay having a peaceful pint when the bully set upon him with disastrous results. The bully was laid low and fisted nearly to death. The townspeople sighed with joy to see him battered by his own brutal methods. They hoped he would die.

For weeks he suffered great pain and lingered on the point of death. When he did die, very few attended his funeral. People protested that he not be buried in the church cemetery.

It was agreed that he was not to be laid there and upset the others, so a hole was dug outside the church tower door. At all costs, he was not to enter Heaven, so a very deep hole was dug and his remains were thrown in and a heavy stone slab was placed on top of him. Should he find a way out, he would go no farther.

The nearest he could ever get to Heaven was to enter the church tower doorway and go up to the ramparts. He was grounded there through eternity.

The inhabitants didn't want him to cause endless trouble in Heaven.

Then one night they saw someone sneaking about. It was his ghost haunting the ramparts, and his only companion was the brazen weather cockerel, which shat on him.

Dyn Tal y Feidr
The Tall Man of the Ghostly Lane

The mile-long and extremely narrow tree-lined lane, with its claustrophobic hedgerows, that leads to St Dogmaels had the dreadful reputation of being haunted by a tall man.

When the river was out, many avoided the lane, preferring to walk along the beach. When it started getting dark, the wind swept down the lane and the trees bent down, resembling fingers thrashing about, trying to catch any foolish person. The raging winds sent chills up and down people's spines, and the possibility of meeting the feared Tall Man had their hair standing on end.

The thought of the Tall Man sent fear through the women, even though many of them had never met him. But the weird tales about him terrified them!

He could appear in the blink of an eye, and his deep breathing froze women inside their clogs. He was suspected of stealing their purses, but what would a spectre from another dimension need money for?

He would lead lonely women far into the darkened upper fields and leave them there to shake and shiver until morning light. Many never recovered from the haunting experience.

There are countless hair-raising tales about this most illusive apparition and many other ghostly goings-on, but the Tall Man had the blame.

A drunken young man with Dutch courage was staggering along one night when he was felled by a hefty blow on his forehead. He slept on the ground most of the night. He rose to his feet with a nasty hangover without realizing he had been knocked out by a floating coffin in a Toili (ghost funeral), with the Tall Man driving it.

Some later night he and his friends looked in awe to see another Toili coming towards them. They jumped onto the hedge to give it passage, and after it had passed, they saw that one of the friends was missing. The Tall Man and his spectral funeral had taken him.

Many had a deep mental shock of terror to be knocked down and then watch in the phantom light as the Toili passed over them. They saw themselves being carried, laid out on top of a coffin. Following behind was another spectral funeral with two naked laid-out bodies on top of a coffin, a warning of their coming deaths.

'Friends, take care, take great care where you tread in the dark! The Spectral Funeral might take you away to places unknown!'

Swnau y Coffin
Coffin Disturbances

As the bearers carried the coffin along the narrow lane leading to the cemetery, a fast running of clogged feet vibrated inside. Six hefty men couldn't hold it still. The inside disturbances rocked the coffin like a boat in a gale.

It rose lightly and then dropped, like a ton in weight, sending the men to their knees. Up and down it went, the inside echoing of running feet dashing in the confined coffin. Enough was more than enough, and the men dropped it onto the roadway so the undertaker could open it for inspection.

The doctor was sent to inspect the dead occupant. He found the passive corpse quite dead and very stiff. The lid was fixed back on, but once the coffin was back on the men's shoulders the furious agitation continued with a vengeance.

Struggling with the distressed coffin, the men managed to get it buried with six feet of earth on top of it. Yet it refused to be still in the earth. The earth mound moved as if a giant mole was heaving about.

The people left the cemetery in a great hurry, as they feared that the corpse might rise and chase them home. What was this presence that was influencing the burial, not wanting the dead person interred there and then buried without any ceremony?

Mam Gwallgof
Demented Mother

A distraught mother had lost her child in the outgoing tide, and later the girl's ghost came back to haunt her. There had been painful years of torment, and the mother took to sleepwalking, searching for her beloved drowned daughter.

From time to time, she was saved from walking over the quay into the outgoing tide by her ever-alert neighbors. But she felt the need to follow her child.

Men unloading a ship of its cargo one dark evening watched with amazement to see the woman with outstretched arms reaching for something, when over the quay she fell. In an instant, two men dived in to save her.

Her husband came to take her home. Later she gave birth to another daughter, and to her delight the child resembled the drowned girl. Gradually, the call of the river receded and she lost her need to go sleepwalking.

She lived to bear six more children, but every week she was seen at the quayside throwing a bunch of flowers into the outgoing tide with the word 'Sally', her lost daughter's name, on it.

Another mother had a young daughter, a princess in her eyes. One day the child was playing with her favorite flowers, the primroses, and without warning suddenly fell dead. Her mother became demented at her loss.

She pined almost to the point of death, and her departed daughter saw her mother's plight. One day the mother saw a vision of a bright and beautiful primrose flower, and behind it was the face of her daughter. The primrose comforted her with its rich scent.

As the years went by, the ailing mother recovered from her wasting sickness. But the delightful primrose remained as fresh as the day it budded. And so it was, until the day she closed her eyes forever, and the ghost primrose vanished.

Llety Bont Godi
The Drawbridge Inn

From the inn in Middle Mwldan, periodic night-fright yells of sheer terror emerged. A woman's agonizing, gurgling gasps and struggles came from the bedroom. They echoed through the night, terrorizing those who heard them.

She was the wife of a sea captain who was on a voyage across the ocean. While he was away, she suffered painful physical invasions. She could see he was in great danger of losing his life.

On this dreadful night, she suffered spasms. In the morning she was found dead in her bed, with the bedclothes in a wild confusion about her. She was half-sitting, half-crouching, her eyes staring at the tilted picture of her husband that hung on the wall at the foot of her bed.

In a nightmare, she had seen her husband fighting for his life as his ship floundered in a great storm. She despairingly reached out to help him, but the terrors were far too much for her heart to cope with, and that led to her death.

Did he? In his last agonizing moments of drowning, did he transmit his thoughts to her and wake her, and yelling at her loss, did she die beside him? With her arms around him, did they die together? Was it possible to drown in bed?

For years thereafter, their ghostly forms were seen strolling arm in arm along the Mwldan waterfront, a lover's embrace in a ghostly romance. Was romance possible after death?

Mam Mam Cei and my poor parents were the 'Show Persons' of our lives. They had passed through the rougher periods of their existence and were often unhappy, yet they found humour. In the gloom of our kitchen, their laughter and homely words of wisdom made for pleasant scenes.

They managed to smile through the most trying of times. We lived in poverty, as did many other families along the Mwldan.

Strolling along the riverside, I saw great beauty in the woods. They were my second home. With my dog at my side—she was my pride and joy—I was able to write our names on the tree leaves. Our spirits rose with the sap to the tree top, and in the next flowering year, our spirits came alive within the tree itself.

It was on one of those occasions that I saw a well-dressed lady making a pretend walkabout looking at the wildflowers. She was a lovely and charmingly cultured woman who stopped once in a while, looking at her expensive gold wristwatch, as she walked past the Pant Cottages and strolled down Lovers' Lane and into Parc-y-Polyn, still looking at the wildflowers. She was on a secret rendezvous.

Walking along the beach was a man who pretended to be out walking and looking at the river. It was all a ruse on his part. Then he disappeared up into the woods, and she entered them, without being seen, to meet him, for rampaging kisses and violent cuddles, in uncontrolled passion.

I and my dog followed them to see what they were up to.

He was very rough and she responded in kisses. They rolled on the forest ground in enjoyment, and it went on for some loveable time. There was no hurry in what they were doing. Soon they relaxed and he lay upon her.

When they got up, he brushed off all the tell-tale marks on her clothes, bits of grass and dust, to make her a respectable looking woman again. Her faced was flushed, though. He made a large opening through the forest for her to sneak back into the lane without being seen.

Her interest went back to the wildflowers, her rampage in the woods kept very secret. As people passed by she gave a nod and a smile and took a leisurely stroll back to Netpool. There was no sign of her candescent lover; he had taken the beach to get back.

It was rumoured that she paid him for services rendered. When I told Mam what I saw, there was alarm in her voice. 'Never mention it to another,' she warned, 'as the blabbermouths could get me into deep water, even to take me to court. You be careful what you tell, what you saw!'

Fanny au Clocs Atsain
Fanny Clogs and Her Ghost Footsteps

She was walking home through the Strand late one evening when she heard footsteps following her, echoing on several different occasions. The first footsteps were her own, and the others, she knew, were departed ghosts of long-lost relations. Why were they after her?

She took no notice until one dark night she heard the echoing sounds right on her heels. They were trying to tell her that something awful was going to happen. She was expecting her second baby any day, so she decided to stay with her sister a few streets away. While she was at her sister's home, the baby came.

On the following day, news arrived that her riverside home was under flood water. Had she been home, she and her baby would have drowned. The night echoes saved their lives. The echoes of the dead had saved the living.

She breathed a prayer. 'Thank you, Mam and Dad!'

Melinydd Llwchus
The Dusty Miller

It is seldom that we are conscious of a connected series of unexpected events leading up to a haunting—until one sees a vague, white-dusted outline of a man covered from head to foot in flour dust.

A dusty miller, a hazy figure, walks hurriedly up and down in front of the mill and suddenly stops, stands, and stares motionless. He looks very agitated as he stares up at some long-forgotten mill windows. He sees someone and raises his right fist, as if to warn or threaten.

For some uncanny moments, this apparition from the past appears to be angry, and those around him see him glaring up at some window. Only they can see the unfolding drama, as he walks along the whitewashed roadside wall.

Someone was hidden in a loft with his precious daughter. He had seen them, and now their illicit affair was out in the open. They refused to give up each other. Smoke came out of the loft window.

Were they ready to burn themselves and the mill?

Cabden y Moch
Captain Pig

This strange and unsavoury character was a wise-acre and a retired sea captain who became an innkeeper. His anger was well known, and the wisest policy was to give him a wide berth.

He kept a piggery next to his inn and told his daft helper to keep the swill simmering all day long, because if the fire went out during the night hours, it took a long time to heat up again.

The lid cover was kept on at all times to prevent playful children from scalding themselves or even falling in, not that he cared. The swill was eaten by the pigs until their bellies bloated out.

Into the simmering swill went anything that was found at the roadside—dead humans, cats, dogs, rats, lambs, fish, whatever. Even drunkards gave body to the swill. This went on for years and years for the best pork around. When the huge boilers were emptied to be cleaned by the captain and his dafter-than-daft helper, the bones were crushed without anyone seeing them, and animal and human skulls were reboiled until they melted into soup. It was the remains of missing people that fattened the pigs, which were slaughtered, salted, and eaten.

It was suggested that the mad captain should commit suicide by offering himself to the simmering swill. Most people were not shocked by his going head first into the swill. They were glad to see the end of such an uncaring monster being eaten by the pigs.

His apparition pointed to his long-time murderous crimes by dancing on the top of the hogwash lid.

His young wife remarried and had a fine brood of upright children who fed on the pigs, of course. For the sake of the captain's relations who still lived around, his evil deeds were kept quiet.

His ghost would be seen running for its life with masses of ghost pigs chasing after to him, looking to eat him!

Dawns y Dal
Dance of the Leaves

The significance of this ritual is now lost in antiquity. As autumn leaves were blown off the tree branches and showered down with the twigs, the twigs were gathered and laid out in a pattern at the base of the tree or trees to form make-believe obstacles to dance about or leap over.

If a child was touched by a falling leaf or twig, he lied on the ground and took no other part of the dance. So it went on until only one child was left standing, who would have a long and prosperous life.

When the frantic winds scattered the leaves, the dances were quickly over and were moved to another part of the woods, where another wide circle of twigs was laid.

The boys took the outer circle and the girls the inner one. In the centre was a third circle of boy-girl-boy-girl, and around and around they danced at ever-increasing speed.

It was a strange Dance of the Circles. The outer circle went clockwise and the inner one went anti-clockwise. The children made leaps over the low edge of the twigs and on landing would clap their hands above their heads.

Joyous girls held hands around a tree and rubbed noses with the tree as they danced around it, laughing hard as they tried to hold their noses to the tree while in motion.

This fair childhood memory is now all forgotten. Perhaps in some dusty archive a meaning can be found for it, something mystical involving fairies unseen, who watched what was going on, representing the present and the future.

Ysbryd y Treath
Strand Ghost

The Strand apparition was a strange one. It wandered in a zig-zag walk and stumbled all over the lane. It was tortuous spectacle.

Weird and unexplainable, it gave fright to the local people, even just to think about it. Those who had to be out in the dark had strange eerie feelings of the dead walking away from the church tombs.

This headless phantom was known to walk about and appear at certain nights of the year. The most frightening thing about its appearance was when it came towards the rear entrance of the Angel Inn. Coming as it did from a distance, its voice echoed behind the person or persons who got nearer to it. They would turn tail and run for their lives; it was better to flee than confront the unseen voice.

In the shrouded mists, no one was sure what sex the ghost was. It wore a long frock, so it could be a priest, a monk, or a woman. One glance was enough for some, and the nearest safe place was past the stables and into the Angel Inn.

Older drinkers there knew what had happened without bothering to ask. No one dared go home the back way; they always left through the front. Many a person out in late evening came almost face to face with the apparition, only to see that it was headless. It went through the person, and many in the morning found that their hair had turned white.

The ghost would be seen in Church Street and then around into the Strand, until it reached the back entrance to the Angel Inn, where it disappeared, dissolving into nothingness.

At least one person, as far as it is known, was struck dumb by that nightly appearance.

Gôl Bach
Churchyard Singer

Gôl Bach was a churchyard singer who wandered between the headstones in the hours before midnight and blew his whistle to inform the interred that he was on his way to sing for them. He heard their silent voices inside his head requesting their favorite hymns and songs. He sang their praises and their beloved one's praises in the dark churchyard.

To him it was the ancient form of paying tribute to the departed and did no one any harm—except that the jealous authorities didn't approve of his nightly transgressions and interfering between the living and the dead. They had skeletons in the cupboard.

He attracted crowds to hear him sing heavenly hymns, and they even joined in, but some guilty inhabitants feared that he might learn something from the interred, of secret family feuds.

Placing pressure on the authorities to curb his unearthly hours and also on Gôl, those residents locked the gates to keep him out. After that, at the hour of midnight, the weather cockerel on the church tower crowed twelve times nightly for a month.

Gôl died within a year, probably of a broken heart. Since the people thought he could commune with the dead, he was not allowed to be buried within the church grounds; he was interred elsewhere, without any minister giving him a religious farewell.

But Gôl Bach seemed to have the last laugh, for at his usual hours, a ghostly heavenly choir echoed among the headstones. He conducted the singers in fine voice into the homes of those who had offended him, giving them no peace of mind. They ran into the cold night streets, the hymns echoing in their heads.

Eventually they went insane and swept the night-time streets between Heaven and Hell. The cockerel sounded the midnight toll for the dead and the un-dead to walk. That was the penalty for the evil ones!

Many parents thought giving their offspring an education and making them use their brains was pointless—they really didn't think their offspring had any brains to begin with. Living with low development was enough to get on in life, nothing more and nothing less. The status quo was ignorance.

There were no indoor toilets in Mwldan. A portable loo was the bucket that was used and then emptied in the river, or buried or thrown unseen early in the morning into an enemy neighbour's back doorstep. Woe betide a child using the night bucket to shit in—he had a nasty beating.

A scared child had to race out in the night and drop it as quickly as a seagull on the wing, in the middle of the road. By day, grass was more plentiful than paper, as hardly anyone used toilet paper unless one was fortunate to have old newspapers and so educate their anuses.

Many a young man, to break the monotony of everyday life, joined the Territorial Army to have a free uniform and be sent away to train. Here was a holiday, as their younger brothers and sisters saw them pack for field training. There were annual parties for servicemen's children, with magic lantern shows, singing and dancing, and stage shows.

There were fireworks displays on Anna Betsy quay provided by a benevolent lady. We were all grateful to her.

Many bonfires were built on Guy Fawkes night, giving people a chance to get rid of old household refuse. Mattresses of straw, alive with fleas, were set alight to float away in the dark outgoing tide. But those special Mwldan fleas were resourceful insects and could swim ashore to find their way back home.

Plentyn Diolwg
The Deformed Bastard

Of all the sorrowful tales we have heard, this one is infused with pathos and compassion.

Two unmarried sisters lived in a cottage in Mwldan. Many years before, one of them had secretly given birth to a deformed baby and kept it out of sight. No one knew about it. Nameless, unable to speak or walk like a normal human, it shuffled around and didn't know the outside world existed.

He was shut in safety and comfort in a back shed that once had been a timber shed. The two sisters tended to his every need. He was harmless and more timid than a rabbit. With the innocence of a young child, he was allowed to roam about the locked-up cottage, sit with them, be nursed by them, and listen to their conversations. But he had such horrible deformities that he grew into a monster.

He understood what they chatted about with intelligence. But being without speech, he was unable to answer them. The years went by quickly, and one cold autumn evening, his mother and aunty went to visit a nearby ailing relative. They made some tragic errors, for in their haste they forgot to lock him in his room, nor did they lock the cottage front door, and left him sleeping with the cat.

Later he woke to find himself all alone. He shuffled about the cottage, uncertain about what to do without guidance. He opened the front door and felt the icy coldness of the chilly wind blasting his face. This outside world was hostile to him.

He dared take himself out into this alien environment. The strange new sounds disturbed him and he was very scared. The wind and rain lashed at him. The wetness of his feet, the shadows, the lower branches seeming to reach down to grab hold of him—all of this made him draw back in a terror that he had never known before.

These fears shook him to the very core of his being. He didn't know where to go. From the inner depths of his heart came a plaintive cry, repeating, repeating, an echoing bleeping for his keepers.

He saw two women in the low mist and thought they were his keepers. As he approached them, he scared the wits out of them, sending them running home. They explained to their husbands that they had been attacked by a fearsome monster. In their overactive imagination and irrational way of thinking, they claimed he had bitten them (but their scratches had come from brambles). 'A wild animal is out there!'

Soon, gangs of men and their vicious dogs went out searching for the monster. Without realising it, the bastard had been going around in circles, and he got trapped. He was viciously clubbed by the men, their dogs tearing at what clothing he wore. He was badly injured and couldn't understand the pain he was suffering.

He managed to flee and get away to some darkened fields, only to be chased farther from the cottage he had known all his life. The trackers were intent to follow him until they had killed him. He swayed and swerved and fought his way through the maze of brambles, making slow progress. At one point, his enemies were almost at his heels. Dogs tore at his shuffling feet. He shouted out wailing cries from the horror and pain being inflicted on him. But from his fear came strength, to escape into the void. He took a tumble and rolled down a steep incline to the estuary beach. The soft sand was a new experience for him. There, his attackers lost track of him.

They searched high and low with lamps, even into the next day. But he had disappeared. Maybe he entered the river, having never seen one before, and was swept away and drowned?

The crazed madmen on his trail cursed that he had given them the slip, as he was almost in their hands. For years, it was the talk of the town.

But the two gentle sisters were in shock at such depravity and held back their tears, embracing each other in grief and loss. No one took any notice as they went about for miles every evening calling *'Babi! Babi! Babi bach ble wyti?'* 'Baby, baby, our dearest baby, where are you?' They wailed through the nights but never found him.

The years took their toll and they died of heartbreak. Even after being laid to rest, the evenings there were far from being silent. Awful guttural wails would rise above the winds, electrifying the night air. Their ghostly haunting cries put a chill in all who heard them. 'Baby, baby, where are you?'

The tenderness of the night went from stillness to silence. Above their empty cottage their apparitions met. On some nights the two sisters would be seen, carrying lamps and searching for their lost child. Their pathetic wailings were never answered.

'Baby, baby, where are you?'

Steps-y-Mwg
The Smoky Steps

The lonely Ladi Wen—the ghostly apparition of the White Lady—is related to the pond or pool on the higher ground above the Old Mill, where the misty atmosphere is icy cold and dank. Dark veils of mist rise under the overhanging trees and a ghostly overgrowth rots in the dark black water.

Ladi Wen haunted here in peace, in a deep feeling of ghostly quietness. One day she displayed herself at the ridge top and gazed down, waiting for somebody or something out of the ordinary. In this dreary scene, dampish above the slate-stone watercourse, she was known as the White Lady of the Mill.

The name of Steps-y-Mwg, or Smoky Steps, comes from what the inhabitants saw in the vapour mists resembling smoke. Some said the name on the wall was Steps-y-Mur, with *mur* meaning wall.

Adar Meirw y Mor
Seabirds Signifying Death

If one chanced to see a single seagull winging above a ship coming in from a voyage, it was a sure sign that one of the crew had perished and the body was under the keel. The deceased's soul was inside the seagull.

Should the gull fly low on the larboard, or port, side, it meant that it was a woman who had died. If it flew to the starboard side, it was sure to be a man, a crew member.

When the ship came to anchor at its home port, the seagull landed on the topmost mast only to fall dead onto the deck. The deceased soul was now free to roam beside the family it had once loved.

Sometimes a group of gulls would wind around the incoming ship. Those were times of apprehension, for they signaled that a whole ship's crew had died, and they were following a safe ship home.

No one ever saw a full group of gulls fall dead, and no one was ever sure that the human souls got free to return to their port or families. Maybe they are still flying around in seagull disguise. Who can tell?

Even porpoises tumbling under the bow or under the ship were protecting the souls from harm. They were the guardians, the angels, of the departed sailors, lost at sea. No fisherman dared to catch or hurt one, and he who was foolish enough to do so perished before he was a day older. He went to the hollow of the un-dead, his ghost or anchored soul floundering in the nether.

Wrach y Dwr
Water Witch

It is most difficult to analyse the ghostly scene. Hysteria electrified the twilight, and parents rushed about in a blind panic in front of the riverside cottages of Bath House, a few feet down from their doors.

The tiny falls could not be seen in the raging flood, and one young girl had wandered too near and was swept away downstream. Her horror screams brought people to see what was happening, and on that fatal evening they saw her going under. As she did, a tremendous crashing movement came through the riverside trees, something large resembling a human bat.

It scooped down and caught hold of the drowning child's hand. In that fraction of a second, all time seemed to stop. It was plain to see that the little girl had been transformed into a beautiful young witch who rose from the flood and flew away. The cold night clouds let the moonlight through, and the girl was seen flying eastwards, never to return again.

Some nights, the cottage inhabitants claimed, they saw a white witch in the sky, circling above their homes. Then in a blink of an eye she was gone. Her once-young parents had aged, but their spiritual strings drew her back from time to time to the place where she was born.

Other children had been taken by the unprotected river, and many distraught parents had recovered their drowned babies and put them in warm ovens, hoping they would recover. But they never did.

Such enduring tales are never far from the hearts and minds of those born and bred in the old Mwldan. One tells of the residents seeing a lone lighted candle searching along the dark streets and praying it would not stop at their front door.

One night, seemingly uncertain as to where it was, the candle rose up to a bedroom window and peeped in. The screams of the child who saw it woke the entire family. They shook and shivered under the blankets, and it gently moved off when the mother shouted at it, 'Go away, you have the wrong house, leave us alone!'

Another night youths went out for some ghostly fun. One sat on another's shoulder, carrying a lighted candle that went out way too often. At one house, he slowly moved the candle from window to window, when suddenly one flew open and a bucket of piss was splattered all over them. They ran off cursing and swearing to the high heavens, their egos smelly with fresh urine. Whoever heard of loud-mouthed ghosts cursing in the night air?

Others thought the candle was carried by an apparition of someone who had drowned in the river years earlier and was now searching for its family that was no more, long ago dead.

But ghosts never age. They have forever lives.

Old Ianto told us tales while we sat on the grass on delightful sunny days. He loved walking about on the sandy expanse of the estuary. He had been told about a wreck of a ghost ship rising out of the incoming tide, with only her forward part and torn sails showing. In it, two sailors were trying to save themselves.

At Pwll-y-Castell (Castle Pool), there was once great excitement when a landmass of reeds and old trees appeared, so thick and wide that it reached from one side of the river to the other. Children would run across it. The phenomenon blocked the river, and ships couldn't enter or leave the port.

It was a mystery that stayed in peoples' memories for generations. People gathered their winter stocks of firewood from it. One time they built bonfires to try to burn it off, until it started to yell and scream. To their amazement, they saw a young sailor who was saved. Many claimed he was a lost relation who drowned as his ship went down.

The smoke from the burning land mass had after-effects. After breathing it into their lungs, people suffered from illusions. Many suffered a temporary madness and frothed at their open mouths. They had nightmares. A great evil had befallen them. A cure was found for their madness. They plastered themselves daily with the river mud for a week, and it worked.

Rhith-y-Gof
The Phantom Blacksmith

Shapes evolve and dissolve to make the inhabitants of Mwldan see odd things afoot. Coming from Parc-y-Felin (Mill Field) into Greenfield Square one night there seemed to be a lone shuffling spectre along the riverside cottages. From that spot, things can look distorted and unreal, but the people witnessed a ghoulish, hammer-carrying phantom blacksmith.

He walked contortedly in a sideways shuffle, his body jerking as if caused by some injury or paralysis. This spectre on the move seemed to prove that life on this earth does not require a living, breathing form of an athlete to exist.

There are ghostly worlds undreamed of in our conscious brains. After all, we are fully dependent on the forces of the spiritual dead, things non-material, that influence us from far and near, are we not?

Standing on the Greenfield Square Bridge, the ghostly figure held a long-handled hammer in his right hand. He looked down river and then in a painfully slow movement readjusted his stance before moving off in fits and starts.

When he reached the entrance back into Parc-y-Felin, he used the hammer to toll the metal and awaken those asleep. He was a despairing soul of the night, an unknown spectre with a past, a rudderless entity disappearing in the low riverside mist, a fascination beyond words.

Now you see it, now you don't.

Clocs y Bont
Upside Down Clogs

One day Mam took us for a walk, and on the red-bricked drawbridge we saw a rowing boat lulled gently out from the slipway. Our attention was on the parapet, and Mam told us to look over, but we couldn't see anything except the lovely watery expanse down river.

She pointed her right hand out from the parapet to show us where the unseen phantom clogs were supposed to hover when the Mwldan River was high. This pair of upside-down clogs hung with their heels toward the bridge, as if some desperate person was jerked out of them in an attempt to drown himself. Whoever it was must have succeeded, as no one came back to claim them.

There was humour in her voice as she told us this, but she stopped when we heard a mighty splash. For a moment, the invisible clogs appeared, and the river was disturbed in a riot of waves as if someone was violently struggling in it. The peace and quiet returned, and the mute swans swam in the calm water.

Dear old Marged Gog (Cuckoo) was a fine conversationalist. She talked out loud twenty-to-the-dozen to her invisible companions. As she ran her fingertips over the inclining hill slate parapet, she told of the person who had leapt off the bridge and left the clogs behind. She had the ability to read the character of those who cut their names in a lasting epitaph to themselves on the flagged slates. She ran her fingertips along the chiseled names and read what had happened to them, learning who they were.

Children made death-defying runs on the narrow flagged top, like circus high-wire walkers showing off with their daring. A few fell over into the river and were saved by their companions. Once a passing undertaker dived in to save one, and by doing so lost a customer.

It was said that people who saw those spectral clogs suspended in mid-air were receiving a sign of a death in the family, so many walkers kept their eyes to the right to avoid seeing them.

Spooks danced under the narrow hill's overhanging oak branches—they were maritime apparitions waiting for the allotted time to go home. While they waited, they rode on the backs of bats to spy on what was going on inside their once-homes, their children fast asleep. Hereabouts the dead live.

Love-stricken maids left their bedroom windows wide open to let the bats suck their blood and reveal the faces of their future husbands-to-be.

Near the top of this narrow Drawbridge Hill, or Rhiw-y-Crogfa (Hangman's Hill), grew a massive oak tree that dropped loads of bouncing acorns onto the hardcore footpath. The acorns would tumble down the hill and accumulate at the bottom, where generations of children picked them up and threw them at Parc-y-Felin's pigs, who grunted in sheer happiness at these acorns, manna from heaven.

Coeden Ladi Wen
The White Lady Tree of Pwllhai

A tall and mighty oak tree on the level below High Street in Cardigan was a most friendly tree. Its branches sheltered generations from the elements. It was the Mighty and Mystical Ladi Wen Tree of Pwllhai, and it was respected and revered.

Those people who touched the tree had a renewal of spiritual vitality. The tree radiated beneficial influence to all who gathered under its spreading branches. Healing rays came up from its roots, from the precious Earth itself.

An old lady living near the tree took precautions not to let anyone injure it. She collected most of the fallen acorns and went about seeding them over a wide area. To her, they were more precious than gold.

This Pwllhai corner was magnetic with cosmic purpose. Those who embraced the tree had an extended lifespan. They felt a sense of natural wonder of the tree's power. It was their Tree of Life.

The ghostly White Lady lived between Heaven and Earth. When people of the lower area died, their bodies were given the privilege of being laid beneath the tree's branches all night, to give them a peaceful entrance to Heaven.

Ysgerbwyd Dan Dwr
Underwater Skeletons

On bright moonlit evenings, people strolling along the bridge often stopped to peep down into the river, mostly from habit, with the faint hope of seeing something floating. Sometimes they saw two white skeletons swimming just under the surface, sometime shoulder to shoulder, other times with one in line behind the other.

The skeletons would drift apart and come together, with one swimming above the other, at high speed. The wonder of it all was that they never surfaced for air, and they made no ripples on the surface. It was as if they were swimming under a cover of glass.

They seemed to appear when there was not a whisper of wind and the tranquillity of the surroundings almost dead. When they went into the shadows, they disappeared, only to reappear in the moonlit clear water.

Some men thought they would have a better look from a boat, but as soon as the boat floated out the skeletons were gone. Some tried to hook them with a hook and line, and once again the surface was disturbed and they vanished. When the wet line was drawn in, the puller received a nasty sting, like an electric shock. The wet line was left there until it dried.

Once peace returned, the skeletons were occasionally seen to resume their underwater frolics. Or were their motives more serious?

Sometimes men from the nearby inns took delight in peeing from the bridge parapet. Once it hit the river, the skeletons were gone. Those peeing lower down on the quayside would feel stings coming through their bodies. One old man remembers the men saying it felt like stinging nettles being drawn up into their insides, a most hurtful experience and never to be mocked again.

It was said that those who saw them were never right in the head afterwards. But there is no proof of this unless one was mad to begin with.

Even from the bridge, people would see vapours in human-like forms drift across the river or float slowly downriver, just brushing the surface...to nowhere.

Ysbrydion Canu
Singing Ghosts

The Singing Ghosts came to life as evening shadows fell. It is never advisable to look into any reflecting surface, like lakes, ponds, pools, rivers, mirrors, or windows when harmonious choral and creepy singing is heard. Their alluring destiny is to capture listeners without being seen—until one fateful moment when the listener foolishly peeps into the reflecting surface and sees them.

There is no escape from the phantom singers, as in their afterlife those who see them are doomed to commune along with them in timeless space, to become eternal songsters.

These Singing Ghosts fill the inquisitive with awe. But at the same time you must steel yourself from yourself, or else you will sing on forever and go out to capture other souls.

The starlit nights are inviting, and the Moon gives extra light, just so you will become a minstrel.

Beware! The night is young!

Ysgerbwd Rhwyfwr
Eel Pool Skeleton

Below Cardigan Bridge, a grim human skeleton was seen on a stormy evening rowing against the fast incoming tide. His ghostly form pulled hard on the oars to force his tiny boat.

Were the Hounds of Hell after him? What was his eager-eerie mission? The fast and furious tide held the boat so that he could not gain nor lose his position. For all his strength and effort, he was not moving.

The river mists and the troubled ice-cold river winds whistled through his exposed ribs, teeth and large empty eye sockets. The awful mist twisted and twirled in sudden gusts. The skeleton and his flat-bottom boat were an awful sight, as all nature was set against him.

Deeper his oars went as out of the mists echoed deep and horrible sighing groans, followed by a woman's high-pitched, stifled screams. It was a distressed lament that echoed from house to house, street to street. Every scream was more terrifying than the one before. Anxious people hurried indoors, to be away from the screaming sensations.

The rowing crazy skeleton paced frantically forwards and backwards as waves splashed at his back. One person found the strength to break away from the spell-bound scene, and another quickly followed in a panic headlong run and missed a footing. He fell into the river and was carried away under the bridge.

The trees hanging above the river were like shrouded monsters. Above them ran the spring gardens roadway to St Dogmaels. But deep underneath the spectre was where the eels congregated to chat about the underworld secrets of the Sargasso Sea, and of the ships and sailors that perished with monsters of the deep, the creeping weeds covering the ships and devouring the helpless sailors until only their skeletons remained.

Had this Eel Pool skeleton been a local sailor trying to row his way home?

The eerie silence of early mornings made a monastic start to my day. I slipped out of the house without anyone knowing. How strange the streets looked without anyone around. The world was at peace, but sadly in many homes there was gloom, stress, and strains, with everyone getting up at the same time, needing to wash and eat breakfast at the same time. It was everyone for himself, and fights would break out.

It was a battleground, with all trying to get ready for school. The smaller children were pushed under the breakfast table, protesting and screaming. Every morning was the same, with children stealing clothes from each other. That's how it was in an overcrowded household, with tears of despair all around.

The mother faced a losing battle to please everyone. She would get the oldest finished first and on his way to school, then the rest in age order: wash, breakfast, and on your way, 'Out!' The same rowdy routine went on up and down the street, with mothers shouting at their children, 'Eat your bread and jam, and go!'

If at times these pages make you smile or sigh, I have achieved my intended purpose, especially the stories of Mam Mam Cei and my mam and their togetherness, their passions, and their hope for better tomorrows.

Cwn Bach y Tylwyth Teg
Tiny Fairy Dogs

A strange flock of birds was seen flying over the River Teifi out of Pembrokeshire, larger than golden eagles. The colour of their feathers was gold and white. In their long narrow beaks were large eggs.

When they were midway between the counties of Pembrokeshire and Ceredigion, an unknown flock of black and grey birds-of-prey came inwards from Cardigan Bay to attack them.

As the golden birds engaged in an air battle, a sudden gale threw them about like leaves in the wind, and they were forced to drop their eggs into the wave-disturbed river. The birds then disappeared, leaving the eggs to crack open to reveal gold and white puppies who did their best to survive. They were saved by the fairies from certain death by drowning.

These tiny river dogs were lovingly brought up and cared for by the woodland fairies, who fed them on sweet nectar. They retained their pretty gold and white chests, which seemed made for living and burrowing under the thorny undergrowth where the fairies preferred to live.

When the full moon reflected in the river, these golden fairy dogs swam alongside the fairies from one side to another and back again.

The long hidden years went by, and one day some of the fairy dogs heard loud shouting and went to investigate. They saw a farmer having some difficulty getting the cattle into a fold.

The dogs thought he was having some fun in a play-around. The concerned fairies called them back, but they were deaf to their calls. They helped the farmer, who had never seen such wonderful tiny dogs.

For their assistance, the farmer gave them bread and milk, which they loved. They decided to stay and help the farmer around the farm. He called them the Cwn Bach y Teifi, for their mysterious appearance from nowhere. They were also called Cwn yr Afon or Cwn Bach y Tylwyth Teg, and, later, Corgwn Afon Teifi (Cardigan corgi).

Rhiw Rhaff-Dalwrn
Ropeyard Hill Apparition

The apparition of a young mother appeared, hurrying along the Rope Walk. Her shoulders were drawn toward the bundle being cuddled in her arms, her shawl covering her baby. Its woolen whiteness glowed in the dark. She was tall and elegant, with a pale face that contrasted with her dark hair, which fell below her shoulders. She was shivering in a lightweight gown not meant to be worn out of doors.

Like the dreadful turmoil of the seas off Cardigan Bay, she moved with a feeling of restless haste, hell-bent on trying to reach her destination. Her feet hardly touched the ground. They were carried along by the invisible wind.

It was a haunting sight to watch the serenity in her flight and plight; it was a scene one could never forget. She showed caution about reaching her impending fate, a pattern of life in the ghostly hereafter.

What could be the reason for the return, year after year, of this Merch-y-Bryn, or Hillside Maiden, and her baby?

Tŷ Tafarn y Cigydd
Butcher's Arms

The inn where the slaughter men came together for a drink was snugly situated in a narrow lane. One of the regular customers was a beastly fellow whose disgusting living habits were unequalled by any ghoul. He never washed or shaved or cut his hair.

He never changed his rotting and stinking clothing. They were allowed to fall off his body. He was a decaying monster and stank to the high heavens. The bits and pieces of decaying animals he had slaughtered stuck about him, and thick blood clots stuck his fingers together.

By day or by night, he stank from a mile away. The odour of death from his presence made all animals run away from him, except for vicious and hungry dogs, which attacked him, thinking he was the bone man. Animals due to be slaughtered died before he got to them.

The town's inhabitants shut their doors and windows when this demonic creature from Hell was near. He sent customers fleeing out of the inn, making them all feel sick by his gangrenous presence. Maggots and worms lived and ate inside his stinking clothing, and some would fall off, to wriggle on the ground.

This most loathsome, ill-mannered creature was being eaten alive by his own maggots. When he finally died, thick coats of tar lined his coffin to keep the stink in and to prevent the insects from crawling out.

For years after, dogs barked and howled at nothing anyone could see, but it was his stinking ghost. His after-death presence made customers flee again. The fated inn finally had to close its doors forever. Then someone burnt it to the ground, and it seemed that the stinking ghost roasted inside it because his haunting stopped.

Will Cot-iar Llygaid Coch
Will the Red-Eyed Moorhen

This amazing man had the ability to see, in any reflecting surface, things like apparitions, happenings of events before they occurred, deaths, etc. Through the years he suffered ridicule and scorn. His name was Will. His red eyes resembled those of a moorhen.

He learnt the hard way that the better part of wisdom was to keep his mouth shut about the premature happenings he foresaw. The ghostly visions were beyond his comprehension.

Will was gifted to penetrate the Veil of Time. He could see strange and unexplainable dimensions, not yet known, of things that delude normal eyesight. Many a time while looking in the mirror shaving, he nearly cut his throat or frightened himself into a nervous breakdown.

He witnessed his own death in his old age. The tears flowed down his wrinkled face. He didn't want to see visions, but they were involuntary and there was nothing he could do about them. As he lay dying, he had a most cheerful smile. He was rosy and healthy looking. Would he be able to change back the years to be a young man again?

Then a broad smile and a wink, and he was gone!

Or had he? What had he to tell them?

Magwyriad y Nos
Night's Invisible Wall

A drunk was strolling down College Row in Cardigan one day. When he turned right into Upper Mwldan, a few yards from Bathhouse Terrace, he found his way blocked by an invisible wall—or was it glass?

He took a running jump at it, but all he got was a flat nose. He kicked it, swore at it, punched it as hard as he dared—and all he got were pains and hurt shoulders. He gave in and turned to walk back the way he came, crossing over the river into Greenfield Square and turning right to follow the river until he reached the Ragged School Bridge.

He turned right to the house where he lived, but before he went in he walked over to the Invisible Wall. It was still in place, whatever it was. Who was able to erect this obstruction in such a short time, and to what purpose?

In the morning he told his friends about the barrier, but they laughed at him, saying 'Put more water in your beer.'

To him, the dead walked lightly, and this ghostly wall was a wall between life and death. Had he been able to crash through it, he would be dead!

Dafi Twpsyn
Daft Dafi

Daft Dafi was a possessed man. He ventured out at night, especially on those with a full moon, hoping to capture one of those illusive White Ladies who had an overriding obsession with his wanderings.

He carried with him a long slender pole that had a large net fixed to the top end of it. He was going to catch one White Lady. According to him, he had some very near misses. He was not greedy—just one would do. Once he caught a white bat. To his reasoning, it was a White Lady who had transformed herself, a very clever ruse, to delude him.

He kept the bat in a cage, where it would have died had it not been for some children and adults out to play a subtle trick. They dressed a young girl in an elegant gown and put her in a large cupboard. When she quietly came out, she walked outside and hid behind a tree and began to converse with Daft Dafi. His heart flutters made him feel weak at the knees.

The hidden girl told him what she had memorized: 'If you let the white bat go, she will turn herself back into a White Lady. She will meet you at midnight at Golwg-y-Mor [Sea View].' Trapped between two disturbing thoughts—to keep the white bat or let it go—he set it free.

At midnight, he was ready to leap over the moon. The night went darker as the moon was lost behind the racing clouds. There a White Lady appeared in her transparent gown. He went to her and they were intimate. (She was actually a paid prostitute.) After years of hunting, his luck had now turned. The Lady of the Night was his at last.

He married her and they had a baby daughter, whom they called Gwen, meaning 'white,' after her mother. Over the years his wife fooled him, always pretending she was the White Lady of his dreams.

He was far too dull to realise the deceit played on him. He would never reveal his candescent meeting with his White Lady of Golwg-y-Mor. And the people living around him had no intention of destroying his fancy dreams.

They all lived happily ever after.

I had a child's outlook on everything colourful and exciting. My demanding summer days there were full of wonder and discovery, pleasure, and adventure.

I loved the enchantment of the riverside sights, the seaweed smells and the odd sounds. I would sit quietly in the hedgerow, spellbound, and spend idle hours scanning the incoming tides for anything unusual. The lovely fields always had the smell of animals, flowers, and odd plants, and the manure pats were sucked dry by multitudes of brown flies. Those evergreens and overgrown plants in the shade were so cool and inviting. Trees had a strange effect on me. I recall the coarse brambles with gnarled hooks and blackberries, summertime at its best.

The coldness of winter meant ponds and riverside frozen over. The white nights resembled the polar regions, and our attic seemed part of the Antarctic. We could be caught up in a freeze while in bed, but the bulky large straw mattress was our igloo and blankets covered us as we slept, sandwiched between them. On chilly evenings we weren't able to sleep after listening to unsettling tales of the unknown. When sleep came, so did my nightmares.

Now in the present, I think about how I was allowed to live this long. Had I known, I certainly would have tried to record the night-time voices of the 'Slate Lovers' who took sexual advantage on our roof slates, and the pissing drunks who cursed to the high heavens, and those who in a wicked temper walked by and lambasted the slates with their walking sticks. Those local characters are now part of my treasured and unforgettable memories of time on the Mwldan.

Dai Ti Mewn, Dai Ti Mas
Dai Inside Out

There are many varied tales of a man who haunted himself. Loud groans and shuffling feet echoed around nine-thirty on a dark evening. Dai heard himself coming down the stairs. It was a hair-raising confrontation as he felt a pulling and a rejection of the person on the stairs. There they were. Dai was outside himself and unable to control the situation.

His dominating self was acting in a happy mood. He danced and stamped his feet in a merry jig. He whirled his body in a fast rhythmic way that seemed out of this world. The music in his head led him on.

Dai tried to control these fleeting emotions and shouted, *'Tawelwch!'* 'Silence!'

The shock of hearing himself shout in a very loud voice gave him a sense of inner calmness and let him regain a sense of reality. But he still couldn't control what was disturbing him, so he held himself rigid.

'Dai, dere I gwely nawr!' 'Dai, come to bed at once!'

As he undressed, his curious wife asked, 'Have you been out in the rain?'

His hair and clothing were sodden by his uncontrolled dancing. His wife did not fail to notice strange things of late about his behaviour. And he didn't tell her anything foolish, because she knew he was already crazy as a coot.

To keep things quiet, Dai had already lost count of his funny turns. But his two selves had a cunning way of paralyzing him with fear. This other self was taking over his life. And who was sleeping with his wife?

In his place was this crazy dancing fool entertaining his wife and children. He sang with the sweetest of voices. He charmed them with laughter that echoed around the house, along with wilder than wild capers. They were all having the best years of their lives, yet he was not with them because this other turbulent character was taking over his fatherly role.

With each passing day, his wife and children joked more and more. He was the family jester.

His other self was having more fun out of life than he was able to, and there was nothing he could do about him. To cap it all, his other self made excellent love to his wife, and she was not able to stop herself from enjoying his sexy ways.

Once he was out in the bay with two other fishermen when they were caught in a nasty gale. They were not far from the shore when their boat overturned. He decided the best course of action was to swim for the shore, but he was not a strong swimmer and the sea was very rough.

Soon he was just swimming to keep afloat, getting weaker and weaker and about to drown. He began having delusions and saw his other self as a most powerful swimmer who said to him, 'If you drown, I'll have no existence!'

The delusion disappeared and went into him, and soon he had the strength of twenty men. He then helped his weakening companions and saved their lives in the powerful currents. No one could understand where Dai got his super strength from.

Dai thanked his other self for saving his life. As they faced one another in the mirror, they agreed there would no longer be a clash of personalities. They jointly became one of two, or two with each other. But then Dai's other jolly self stepped out and left the physical Dai alone inside the mirror!

Without knowing it, the most contented and happy wife had two men in her life: the physical Dai and the vibrant ghost, to please her every need. The wild music and dancing went on and on.

Kitchen nights were claustrophobic, with neighbourly women calling in to have chats and give accounts of their daily lives, pastimes, loneliness. Their individual voices were special moments to remember. It was a wonder how they managed to keep life and limb together, yet still keep their humour.

Large families in overcrowded 'one-up, one-down' homes with hardly any furniture had rough, tough times trying to manage in poverty. They often suffered from tuberculosis, TB, a deadly infection with a lingering death. The infected would sleep with the heathy, eventually leading to the whole family suffering from the disease.

Conditions were unsanitary. The bucket used for night toilet stank of stale piss. Many slept on the floorboards as there was no room for hulky mattress beds. Those were heavily flea-ridden, and rats would chase about and be bitten by the very fleas that had feasted on the children.

Families constantly faced ill health and impending death, but it was part of living in the Mwldan. Funerals were frequent. The dreaded undertaker was a regular caller in those streets.

Many people had a strange habit of thrashing the dead. Some thought that by beating the coffin with green twigs that they could take away all the sins committed by the deceased and dislodge the evil spirits housed inside, releasing earthly sins.

Did it work?

Cwilt Wraig
Quilt Widow

This is the unfortunate tale of a much-loved and humble old widow and master quilt-maker. She made wonderful, out-of-this-world creations. But she was poor and existed entirely from earnings from the quilts she made and sold.

She was called 'Cwilt Wraig Pentan' due to the fact that she spent her declining years near the fireside, where she laboured on her extra-special designs, hoping to sell one so she could buy coal for her fire before the winter months set in. Any money left went to buy more fabric.

Her neighbours admired the quilts beyond words, and her best creations sold quickly. She always took people by their word. One day a wealthy family in the town promised to pay her the next day for quilts they bought. For weeks, she had starved herself in her cold kitchen to finish the quilts, unable to think about the money she would have tomorrow. She deserved it—had she not starved?

The next day she went to their house to get her money, but no one was home. The next day, and then the next week, went by. She would meet the family members in the street and ask for her quilt money, but they ignored her and refused to pay her, not one red penny.

One day, weak and with a heavy heart, she collapsed in the roadside and her caring neighbours came to carry her home. The wealthy family members smiled as she was taken away from the front of their elegant house. They had taken her quilts and now it seemed they were taking her life as well.

They had betrayed her by accepting her woollen creations, her labour of love. The effects of long-term hunger forced her to bed. Each passing day seemed her last. She refused charity from even her best friends. Even when others owed her money, she preferred to die rather than accept a morsel.

Concerned neighbours went to speak to those who stole her quilts, but the upstarts refused to listen. Soon the widow died. Breathing her last words she uttered a curse; her quilts would avenge her death.

A large crowd gathered at her funeral, and afterwards her neighbours gathered in silence outside the quilt thieves' home, as a nasty tribute to their evilness.

For a few weeks after her funeral, nothing happened. When the nights grew colder, the thieves put their ill-gotten quilts on their beds. Then the ghostly quilts went on the move.

The first incident began with the husband suffering from crazy nightmares that grew in intensity. His wife was not able to sleep, and she soon saw visions of the quilts changing into hideous creatures that crept heavily over their bed.

The heavy trampling of feet on the bed made her husband leap out and shout to his wife, 'Get out!' *'Talwech hi!' 'Talwech hi!'* The haunting words echoed inside his head. 'Pay her!' 'Pay her!' But it was not his voice but a deep-throated presence. The ghost haunted the woman so much that she couldn't take it anymore. The following day she was missing, and later she was found on the riverside. She had drowned herself.

Her formidable husband thought he was made of sterner stuff. But he was the next victim of the quilt's curse. The heavy quilt pressed down on him and over his face, and he died of heart failure. His children were quickly taken to live with their uncle, with hopes they'd be safer there.

But their aunty woke one night with a quilt around her throat strangling her. Scared out of her wits, she hurried to get a glass of water to drink. In her haste she fell headlong down the stairs and broke her neck.

Her husband found her with the wasted apparition of the quilt widow standing beside her. She held her hand out to him, and he fled in terror, pursued by the ghost. He ran into the stables and hung himself from the rafters. Once again, the children were moved to another address.

Another family relation, as it turned out, had one of the widow's quilts covering their children's bed. The father realised something terrible was about to happen. On investigating he found that their daughters had been smothered to death by the quilt. His guilt was such that he was found later in the fields, his head blown off. He had killed himself.

His frightened wife ran off and was never seen again.

Another guilt-ridden relation was on guard in his home one evening, fearing the worst could happen to them. It was a cold night, so he made himself a fire in the grate. His only daughter was asleep with a quilt covering her bed. He gazed into the fire and fell asleep in his chair. He woke up to see in the silence some strange and horrible creatures haunting around him; they were hideous decaying depravities.

Loud drumming noises were made by the tramping of heavy feet. The floorboards bent under their weight. Enough was enough, and he ran to the door. It failed to open. The ghostly presences were brooding, threatening.

When daylight came, he faced another tragic shock. His precious daughter was dead. She had died in extreme terror, her mouth wide open expressing horror. The quilts had taken their toll once more.

Later a quilt covering his bed had terrible consequences. He woke up to find a haggard and decomposing old widow in bed beside him, her decaying breath on his face. With one mighty leap, he jumped out of bed and crashed through the bedroom window, breaking his neck. The avenging quilts had finally taken the entire family.

The quilts were given to the poor Mwldan families, and their children suffered no ill effects. The quilts became precious heirlooms and were passed from one generation to the next. Sad to say, this tale of the poor Cwilt Wraig remained forgotten in the annals of Mwldan.

Until now.

The gloomy kitchen was the threshold of our spiritual beings on earth. My brother and sisters were nurtured within its walls, seated there in the shadows. Was our birth a matter of chance, a ghostly cause? Ghostly presences control our destinies. They make us out as they want us to be. The Mwldan question was, 'Is there a purpose to our lives?'

The dark candle-lit fireside was like a wonderful and illusive cavern, enchanting in an infinite variety of moods. Mam in her sweetest temper and merry voice explained things to us. However much we tried to understand the ghostly atmosphere, the fear of the unknown kept invading our lives.

Ghostly figures in monk-like habits were seen coming through the rear double doors of 17 Quay Street. They would float or stroll effortlessly, in a meditative mood. After a while, one after another, they would turn about and finally disappear back the way they came.

It was no wonder that the bare-bummed stone-age chickens had their backs and rear ends without any feathers, flashing their red-raw bums as the ghosts kept riding and racing them around Lower Mwldan. To stop they had to skid on their bare bums.

Rhith-y-Ffynon
Water Spirits of the Well

One of the oddest sights in old Cardigan was that of an elderly woman who in her younger days had had charm and beauty. An apparition, she would rise out of the meadow at a secretive Moon Time.

She was a lady of great importance who had lived in a grand mansion with her daughter. They lived alone except for a few maids to look after them. One day, the old lady became very ill and on a moonlit night took herself out for a stroll into the meadow, where a magic well had been known for generations.

Into the well she dropped, and swam the best that her strength allowed. One of her elderly maids, who was keeping an eye on her, feared at what she saw and ran back to alert the daughter. 'Your mother is in the well!'

The well was searched and also the surrounding land, but the woman had disappeared off the face of the Earth. The concerned daughter, who had felt obliged to watch after her mother, never got married or had children. Because of her guilt, she sacrificed her happiness. With all hope gone, she resigned herself to be a lonely old maid.

Her mother had been her priority. The stress of her disappearance became unbearable. One night she made her way to the well and fell headlong into the deep cold water, splashing into the darkness. But instead of finding death, she became vibrantly alive and in the prime of maidenhood. Without much effort, she pulled herself out of the well.

She sat in the fresh air and thought it was all a fantastic dream, to be an energetically alive as a young girl of eighteen, walking in the air. On her return to the mansion, she brazenly walked in and faced stern old Margaret, one of the maids, who refused her entry.

'Who are you?'

'I have come to visit my aunty,' the girl replied.

She walked smartly past the old housemaid to reach her room, where she quickly changed out of her damp clothing. It was then she saw herself in the mirror. The shock hit her. She saw she was young and beautiful, what a wonderful surprise. But soon all the bucks in the area would be after her.

On the next full moon, she took old Margaret with her into the meadow. When they got to the well, she gave the woman a push, and she hit the cold dark water with a mighty splash. The girl shouted down to her, 'Use the rope to pull yourself back up.'

Margaret came up as a vibrant eighteen-year-old girl. Her heavy work clothes hung about her, and soon she was naked in the moonlight. The two girls ran about like goddesses of the night.

But where was the mother?

The months went by and young-old Margaret married a wealthy landowner and lived happily with a family. The secret of the well was safe with them.

And could they cheat old age?

The loveable nymphs emerged as two slight young girls. The well water was their chrysalis. They had an obsession to marry and have as many children as possible. They outlived husband after husband and many, many children. The well was their Shangri-la.

They lost count how old they really were. The centuries rolled by, with all their unforgettable rebirths. They protected the well and made it out of bounds to people who once had been able to occupy its wooden seats.

But as time went by, their modern-day offspring need to till the land for agricultural use and so had the well filled and the land ploughed.

Those responsible for this crime were dismissed and disinherited, but the entire estate was later sold to strangers. Now, at long last, the women were mortal. Their ghosts could be seen at a special full moon, two old and infirm old ladies seated on their favourite bench. Roaming about by day were young children, and the ghosts were the grandparents of them all.

The full moon knew the secrets of the well, and it wasn't talking.

One sunny, delightful day, I was with Mam Mam Cei and Mam at the corner steps off Spillar's Quay. I was told not to go near the slippery steps. Mam Mam Cei was standing alone, looking wistfully downriver to St Dogmaels, the village where she was born.

The incoming tide lapped noisily in the wall joints. It was a glorious and peaceful sight. But she had a strange tired look in her eyes. What was she thinking about?

A riverside mystic with a sad expression, she had a faraway stare, lost in a world of her own. Her grandchildren were racing about and laughing, but the tide was coming in, making it dangerous for us. Off we went to the quay of Anna Betsy. The two women sat on the wooden bench and got to chatting until they decided it was tea time. Off we drifted to our own homes, just around the corner.

I loved our old home, and I value those years it gave me and my family shelter from the elements, as well as the countless years of pain, joys, and sorrows. It was a budding part of our individual personalities. Its rooms were the blank pages of our lives. Am I now a sentimental old fool?

The kitchen is where tales of old brought about my interest in trying to record all I heard there. I felt safe in those strong walls, alongside by brother, Willy. It was the book of our lives.

In considering the past, I recall how often one can be taken by surprise. One day we learned that Mam Mam Cei was ill. I had not seen her for some time. The homely quietness in our home crippled our lives, as we waited for a recovery that never came.

The loveable mystic who brought us magic, Maria Morgan, died on March 18, 1934, at the age of 73.

I didn't think mortality had anything to do with our lives until that happened. Mam felt the loss more than words can say. And when she took me to see Mam Ma Cei in her coffin, so still, I felt sick at seeing her dead. I now wish Mam hadn't, but Mam needed to see her. It was my farewell to her, and I watched as the tears rolled down Mam's face.

Our home was not the same without her. Her tales had lit our kitchen with her vividness. She passed along the old beliefs that had been passed to her. The kitchen was our contemporary theatre. It would be impossible to calculate how many impressions she left us with. She was an ageless magician who changed our outlook on life forever.

We never cease to mourn her, but we have the legacy of her wonderful tales. We will remember her cheerfulness, her wisdom, and her contented outlook on life. She was never hasty in her decisions, and in her quiet way never struggled for self-expression. She had the precious gift to be amusing. She hated false moods in people who were out to get their greedy ways.

She loved us very much and always kissed us before leaving. After 'lifting the anchor,' she and Mam took a short walk to her home.

'Blod, mae amser I cod'r angor!' 'Blod, it's time to lift the anchor!'

Time to get the wind into one's sails. Her home became a rudderless one as her life in the Mwldan came to an end. She was ready to raise her sails and go with the tide into the sunset of Cardigan Bay, to Heaven.

Matri Bach
Tiny Matri

She was a small, beautiful, and fragile girl, who against the strong advice of her loving parents, married a beast of an unfeeling man and lived to regret it. Her life was one of perpetual assaults; he was a wife beater, and her only joy was her faithful dog, which her husband took a disliking to.

One day the dog went for him as he assaulted his wife. He grabbed the dog by the scruff of its neck and went to the quayside to drown it. But another dog came to attack the dog held by the man. As the dogs fought under his feet, he cursed aloud, and soon the three of them got tangled and tipped over into the river.

Wet and shaken, the dogs swam ashore and made their way home. The drunken man sunk to his death. Instead of a respectful funeral, the people had a happy celebration. In the cemetery, the coffin was turned upside down to make him eat dirt.

The dogs had a grand party and later were well looked after. They had the freedom of the house, and they made sure the man's ghost never came home to haunt the wife. Once, a pale face was seen peeping through the window. The dogs went wild and chased the damned ghost back to his coffin.

They all lived in luxury, and fat-bellied the dogs slept where the man had slept, with everyone in excellent spirits.

Dilys-y-Gwynt
Dilys of the Wind

It is a fact that women were more gifted in the paranormal. Dilys of the Wind had an uncanny talent to read what was in the winds. She had powerful perceptions and could see ghosts travelling about in the winds or in the wind caves on the beaches.

She was a bright and wizened old lady with an active intellect. She was often seen sitting under a tree in meditation, or strolling softer than a cat through the woods. The wind was sending messages to her—every sound through the tree was a message, down to the branches and shaking leaves.

In her home, drifting breezes and draughts told her of strange happenings about. She was attuned to understand their strange interpretations. The ghosts danced in a circle, and soon she would be in a field beside them.

Worried people came to have ghostly consultations with her. She gave them a cure for 'Pen Tro,' a giddiness brought on by being out in the winds. She sat beside them and would let the winds speak, sometimes in concert.

Mesmerized and breathing low, she received messages in the breezes. She was able to divine the future and was quite knowledgeable. It was remarkable for one so old. She was an ageless genius.

She didn't die in the ordinary sense; her remains simply dusted away in the winds. Her soul made its home in the high trees above the village of Llandudoch (St Dogmaels) after the life of Dilys ended.

Mor-Forwyn
The Mermaid

Another unusual woman had the nickname of Siwen or mermaid (*mor-forwyn*). She had her own special powers to divine the movements of the sea. She was often seen standing out on the edge of the cliff and challenging the winds to blow her to her doom.

The surging waves were clashing-dashing on the jagged rocks to create huge clouds of white froth. Careless, at the height of madness, she stood firm trying to control all she viewed. She wished to master the tumultuous ocean. She felt conflicting passions as the raging waves tried to reach her.

Flying clouds of foam larger than elephants blew inland and changed shapes and patterns. All were creature-like clouds hoping to push her into the raging inferno.

But out of the turmoil she was able to understand what Nature was revealing to her and her alone. Siwen was the mistress of the oceans and all she saw.

In adverse weather conditions, we were to be found in our kitchen, in deep conversation and communing with the ghosts. Those who told the tales 'scared' the rest. The focal point of interest was the bright corner glow of the fire. This night we were alone.

No one in his right mind would be caught outside as the deluge pelted savagely down. The river was in a spate, swollen, and the wild winds whistled and the thunder echoed, vibrating down the chimney and breaking loose large lumps of soot.

Mam's melodramatic stories made us smile. She would take on a child's voice and think as a child. With the raging storm tearing the outdoors to pieces, her eerie stories added further effects. Any second, a storm ghost the size of an elephant might come down the chimney, or a skeleton would stand upright and rattle his bones, shivering from the cold night.

We were eventually sent up to our attic bed, to hear the wind and rain lashing on the slates. The low bit of candle would go out and the weather would lull us to sleep.

Tywod yn Canu
The Singing Estuary Sand

When people would wander along the estuary beach looking for driftwood or whatever they could find for their home fires, or collect shellfish and seaweed for a meal, the seeping in the sands began to sing. It was a sort of music the fishermen feared.

'Pan bod y tywod yn canu mae melltith yn a gywnt!'
'When the sands sing there is tragedy in the wind!'

When the dreaded low wind blew over the sand, it sang and foretold of troubles to come—of deaths and shipwrecks. They say it is an ill wind that blows no good, and some people walking the sands heard of unspeakable roars, screams, and warnings of misfortunes to come. The wind sands raced around kicking up miniature whirlwinds.

Concerned women would give sound advice not to trust the river or the sands due to the order of things. The incoming river would silently surround the unwary playing on the estuary, and there would be no escape except by boat or by swimming out, if one was a strong swimmer. The sand would sing their doom.

One St Dogmaels lady claimed she had a secret of a devilish poem and wouldn't dare let anyone read it. She swore on her Bible that those who did would fall ill and die not long afterwards. The poem was kept in her bedroom, wrapped in strong brown paper. Whenever she moved it, she wore gloves so as not to touch it. One day she feared that members of her family might touch it and receive the 'Touch of Death.' So she sealed it in a strong box and hid it in the dark corner of her attic.

In time it was covered by spider webs and forgotten.

Mam Mam Cei advised us, 'take great care if you should ever find a sealed tin box. Leave well enough alone, for it may turn out to be a Pandora's Box. I never want to see misfortune be your lot.'

Being born in Cwmdegwel in the village of St Dogmaels, she knew all about the Singing Sands and the dreaded tin-box. It was from her we learnt about the 'Ghosts of the Seas', the mermaids who were taken for granted since no one ever saw them. But many fishermen had heard their haunted singing. Their voices echoed from Trwyn-yr-Olchfa and Cemaes Head, and as they rowed quietly in and out of Pwll Emlyn, Pwll Edrych, Carreg Llydan, Ogof Groyn, Carreg Aderyn, and Pwll Mwn, the half-human, half-fish. Their expressive melodies had intellectual charm, the mystiques of Cardigan Bay.

Coastal areas like Cemaes Head were likeable settings for their unseen haunts. They were never far from the submerged lost city of Cantref Gwaelod. Were they responsible for tolling the bells heard from the shore?

Local myths give a fairly good foundation to the bizarre. Who can deny the wonderful mysteries that dominate our ancient coastal heritage? Tales of these lovely sea maidens have been brought down through generations by word of mouth, and from these strange sources we come to remember them. It will be a sad day when we no longer do!

Hen Wraig Pentan
Chimney Corner Hag

She told eerie tales of the unexpected that were so entrancing. She charmed all who listened to her. Every time the wind blew smoke back into the kitchen, she saw it as some sort of ill-omen. She wobbled like a loose leaf in the wind and startled us by turning into smoke herself.

The sudden smoke cloud blew back to burn our eyes and make them water. She was now without a stable form. She changed into a smoky spectre and was pulled back up into the chimney.

Many sane families refused to admit her entrance into their homes or hear her fantastic tales, as to them she was a crazy fool. But in our home she was an entertaining woman of great talent. She was full of energy and could dance and sing cheerful songs, and she made us sing along with her.

She refused to eat or drink.

When she heard of a farmer who ill-treated his dogs, she was so annoyed that she changed the cruel farmer into a dog, and the dog into the farmer, for a month. After that, the farmer learnt a bitter lesson not to abuse the animals under his care.

She, the chimney corner hag, was to us a very delightful ghost, our Lady of the Night.

Twm Ffagod
Twm Faggots

Twm Ffagod, or Twm Faggots, was his nickname because of his favourite meal of faggots. One day something had infuriated his wife, and she shouted her opinion on Greenfield Square, where they lived.

'Dim ond un Diafol sydd mewn Uffern ond mae un ar pen pob heol yn Aberteifi!'

'Hell hath but one Devil, but Cardigan Town hath one on every street corner!'

Cannwyll Corff
Corpse Candle

These psychic manifestations attract and arouse unfolding interest into the Mwldan spectres. They appear when people least expect them.

Corpse candles are no exception because they are seen floating mid-stream in the outgoing tides, never inwards. They are always women. When people research the phenomenon, they get confused and have a feeling of hopelessness. They experience the sheer horror of what might come with them — a ghost!

Not far from where Twm Faggots lived was the old Tannery Building. It was reputed to be haunted.

The ghost in the loft above was seen with a Corpse Candle in his hand as he rode an old penny-farthing bike. It plonked rowdily over the loft boards. The candle would go out and then alight again as he raced across the empty loft.

With great vigor, the ghost belted along on his bone-shaker. It was a speedster without brakes, and he was a road-hog who rode faster than a motorbike. A gang of boys out in the dark road threw stones through an open space where a window had once been. The stones bounced inside—the boys' hope was to give the rider a bump on the head. To everyone's (make-believe) alarm and surprise, a blurry pale face looked out. There was no waiting about; the boys scattered like scared rabbits, tumbling over each other.

Opposite the building was the Steps-y-Mwg, where the ghostly woman, the Ladi Wen (White Lady), lived. The two ghosts chased and tipped over the boys, who fled blindly. They got safely home and never challenged the Tannery Ghost with stones again.

Llety Hyddwen
White Hart Inn

Dan Erlyn, after a few pints of beer, stepped into the roadway of St Mary Street and was involved in a ghostly accident. He was run over by horses and coach. He felt the hooves pound on top of his body and felt the crushing of his bones. He saw the underside of the coach as it passed over him, his life ebbing away in the darkness.

The distressing experience of dying on the roadway numbed him as he lay prostrate. His friends inside the inn heard loud shouting and the neighing of horses. They came out to investigate, only to see Dan on the road. But they could not understand what the fuss was all about, because drunken Dan rose to his feet.

The next morning, for some unknown reason, he was black and blue. He had relived himself in another lifetime, only to be nearly killed again on that very spot. His ghost was making him relive the accident all over again.

He sat down. The strain was too much to think any more that day.

Later, sitting in the White Hart with two pints in front of him, with his ghost alongside him, he drank a good health to both of them. After some time, he got up and told his ghost to go out first, explaining that if he got run over, it didn't matter since he had no bones to break nor life to lose. Then Dan went out by the back entrance. There was a method in his madness.

High above behind our attic bedroom was the hulking, magnificent, and derelict Old Market building, still prominent in its neglected state above the quays and the river.

Once, unseen, I sneaked inside and wandered through the hollow-sounding lofts. I was a lone explorer discovering something new out of old things. It had been the town market place and was now housing the ghosts of the workers. From the top loft, I was the master of all I surveyed. It was a nice place to kick a ball across the lofts, especially on a rainy day.

But those empty lofts gave me feelings of loneliness and deep pathos. I must have been one of the last to peep and reflect on all that had been. I scratched my name on a slate window sill. The lofts were a place to sit and dream.

Even though the building was empty and unused, there were some men who got a lot of satisfaction in thrashing any boys trapped inside. Yet nothing was said about those vandals who ripped up the floorboards for firewood.

Once a man came in to look about and I rushed to hide under some rotting sacks left in a corner. The sacks stank of dust and pigeon and rat droppings. Hardly breathing in the dreadful smell, I lay very still and silent, until the echoing footsteps stopped.

When the trespasser began to tear up the floorboards, I shouted at him from above. He couldn't tell where the sound came from and took to his heels, leaving behind an almost new axe.

The top loft was my favourite, because I could hear the heavy rain on the roof, the wind rattling on the windows, and whistling howls making tiny tornadoes that would twist and turn and create dust clouds, swirling old leaves over the floorboards.

It was my secret wish to have a bed up there, one massive bedroom. It could become our home, a healthier abode than the cabin-size bedrooms along the Mwldan. The up-draughts sounded like the haunting echoes of souls in distress. Were the Powers of Darkness waiting?

It was once a wonderful building, but now it was a place where the past was in a losing battle with the present. I was part of that loss and change, a witness to a monster that had outlived its intended usefulness. It was now a secret playground. Was it also at night a place for secret illicit lovers?

I would climb out without being seen, stepping down the splendid slate stairway into Market Lane, then climbing down the steep incline wall to the large double green doors and dropping into the yard. I raced indoors for the tea Mam was preparing.

Dial y Morwr
Sailor's Revenge

Outside the hulking Market Building and on the square was a granite statue of a ghostly horse, petrified to death by the spectre of a young sailor who haunted the lofts. Seeking revenge, the sailor struggled in his rusty chains on his hands and feet.

The chains echoed as he dragged himself across the wooden floor of the loft. He became especially agitated when the tides were running inwards, bringing storms and torrential rain in from the ocean.

He went into terrible and uncontrollable rages, smashing the chains that bound him on the loft's walls and heavy oak doors. He would have his revenge on the unfeeling captain who brutally murdered him on board his ship.

The captain was not in his ship on the high seas. He was in the empty lofts of his once-thriving business. He was trying to slay the young man's ghost, his cutlass slashing, but there was no one there, just the empty air.

In the lofts the two were playing a game of cat and mouse, with the captain being taunted by painful cries, to try to break his resolve. When the ghost's anger was let loose, a member of the captain's family would perish. Hell hath no fury like a young ghost scorned!

The spectre wilted down the captain's family with terrible inflictions, without mercy or sanctuary for any except death. The brutal captain would be the last to go.

The happy spectre sat on the window sill, swinging his legs, so that the chains echoed about to fool the crazed captain. He jumped about in twists and turns, with his sword swishing noisily. He rushed outside, forcing the neighbours to bolt themselves behind their front doors. But he chopped on their doors because he thought they were harbouring the young man's ghost.

He didn't stop even when buckets of excreta and piss landed on him.

The young ghost was in no hurry to end their conflict. He had all the time in the world.

Cor y Lon
The Midgets of Ebens Lane

Crammed into the corner was the smallest house in town. It was made for tiny people. Seated on the top front door step, the inhabitants watched their neighbours pass by. It was a tiny one-up, one-down, a derelict reminder of a doll's house. Every now and then the tiny pair, a husband and wife, greeted the passers-by, *'Hi roes iti, Will!'* *'Hi roes iti, Jane!'* 'Long life to you, Will!' 'Long life to you, Jane!'

The husband dropped from one step to the next to reach the road on his short legs. He was unable to walk quickly but he had the speed of a weasel. His name was Twm Carlamu. He could move like a Jack-a-Jumper and leap about.

I loved climbing into high tree branches and seeing cattle, horses, and sheep grazing in the fields. There I was nearer to heaven (if there is such a daft place) than those fervent chapel goers whose preoccupation was spreading awful lies while they stank to the high heavens of camphor and death. They were the Walking Dead.

I noticed how very pious they were on Sundays as they prayed to God. They tried to look meek and mild, but during the week they made a violent change, swearing and cursing worse than the devil. We children took the brunt of them. They would natter all day and night, quoting in parrot fashion with missionary zeal.

Their devout Christian upbringing was nothing more than spiritual slavery. For shopkeepers, the holy voice of God was in the tills, ringing, 'Ma Iesu yn siarad yn y till.' 'It's far better to have cash in the till than religion, and God and Jesus are ghosts themselves!'

Mari Fach was a curious woman who would pester the preacher. 'Who placed the sun in the sky?' 'Who lit the skies?' 'When was the first hour?' 'Who gave us eyes to see?' Irritated by questions he wasn't able to answer, the preacher would call out to her, 'Get away from me, you old fool. You need to see the witch doctor.'

'Will she give me reliable answers, and where can I find her?'

Pwll Dafi
Dafi's Pool

The way in which Dafi met his death remains a mystery. There are many different versions floating about. One is that he and his faithful horse, and their loaded cart, disappeared into a deep, murky pool on the left side of the road not far from Pont-y-Cleifion.

When the high winds blow and sigh through the branches of the tress that line the roadway, Dafi's apparition can be seen, sitting on his cart in those fateful bygone years. Was it an accident or not?

Who can now know the truth since all the evidence lies deep in the hard-pressed sediment that was once a watering hole for the animals. Eventually, through neglect, it became a pool of no return. The bodies of Dafi and his horse were never recovered.

When Dafi took to his usual drinking habits, he relied on his well-trained horse to take him home. But on that day, in a heavy rain, Dafi left the town's stable with his horse and loaded cart, drinking out of a flagon and headed out of town.

As they neared the pool, which was heavy with flood water, his horse needed a drink. Having drunk his fill, the horse found that the weighty cart refused to reverse out of the slippery side. The more the horse struggled, the deeper into the pool the cart slipped. Dafi was too drunk to realise the danger he was in. He was deaf to the maddened neighs of his horse, and, doomed, they went under without a trace.

That explains the accident—or does it?

How did it become to be called Pwll Dafi if no one saw him perish…unless there was a sinister motive?

A strange atmosphere hovered over the pool. There seemed to be a presence that intrigued the inquiring mind. But there were certain 'silent' objections to people who wanted to excavate the fatal watering pool, for reasons unknown.

Dafi's ghostly appearance revealed, with a flagon in his hand, that he and his horse were sent to their prearranged deaths. The trees were witnesses to his disappearance. He sang out what happened: He didn't perish as we had been led to believe; he was murdered for the contraband in his cart.

The tall trees knew. They sang of Dafi's unhappy fate. Dafi's voice also rang loud in the winds that echoed in this lower part of the town, telling of his killers and what really happened to him.

Certain of the town's individuals had a way of obscuring the past. They had the original trees destroyed and so silenced the mystery.

Is this the last of Dafi's tale of woe?

Eyllyll y Ffynon
Elf of the Well

A hideous elf concealed himself in the green shadows surrounding the riverside well. He had broad and mighty shoulders, and in his right hand he clasped a club, ready to lay low anyone foolish enough to vandalize the well of Lover's Lane.

The name was a misnomer, as it was not a well but a spring with a flat stone at the bottom for people to stand their buckets on while the waters slowly filled them. To reach it, there were stepping stones to keep one's footwear dry.

It was hidden by ivy and other fresh-water-loving plants, and for some reason lots of white pebbles and seashells were placed all around by generations of children—little piles left as homage to the Water Spirits.

The cold drinking water was full of mystery and magic and healing properties that cured blindness and other unspecified illness.

Vandals quenching their thirst were infected by terrible visions coiling about them of monster snakes about to strike at their faces and swallow them. Some struggled and shuffled about with clubbed feet as long as the visions lasted, often for a few days. These vandals paid a rough price for their stupidity.

The elf was well camouflaged, and only his eyes could be seen looking around. He was weirdly dressed in a tight green cloth that had turned white with centuries of wear and tear. The mighty elf was ageless.

Children never stayed longer than was necessary to quench their thirst; they used the ivy leaves as cups. By the time they climbed out into Lover's Lane, they were shivering from an icy feeling. The 'Well Way' was their shortcut to the beach, but it was the home of myth and legends and of the unseen green-clad Ellyll.

The elf, or goblin, could materialize when the vandals came to cause damage to his secret abode. There was little room in the narrow footpath to riot when his vision appeared among them as a prehistoric monster. They thought it appeared out of the earth, ready to swallow them.

Fear-ridden, they leapt off the shoulder-high well-wall into the high tide, swimming as fast as they could to reach the slipway in safety. Beside the Pant Cottages, they ran off.

Y Diafol Coch Dawnsiwr a Ladi Wen

The Dancing Red Devil and the White Lady

As the grey evening light grows dimmer and the mist covers the riverside area, a timeless ritual begins. The Ladi Wen, or White Lady, wearing a light veil that covers her elegant body, lowers herself out of the topmost branches of the Cryptic Oak to stand on the hill below. Her hand signals for the rock face to open, and the tree shakes and vibrates to reveal a tunnel to an underground cavern.

Out leaps a very bubbly-energetic and loveable rascal in a red glow of satanic splendor, lighting up the top of the Drawbridge Hill. This fickle red-dancing Devil is locked away and out of sight by day within the deep root system of the Cryptic Oak. From above, the Ladi Wen guards his comfortable abode, as he is a very, very special Devilman to her!

He jumps off the ledge into her waiting arms, and they embrace and dance in a fast jig down the hill to the drawbridge and back up the hill, then on to the flat ground into Netpool and down to the Slipway besides the Pant Cottages, and up the short hill behind the cottages to reach Lon y Cariadion (Lover's Lane), past the Old Well as far as the entrance to Parc-y-Polyn (Pole Field) and back and forth through the night.

In a passionate embrace at the Slipway, they dance a wave jig in the high tide to cool their feet. At dawn they come to their last and final dance below the sacred oak, in a blurred-whirl of passionate embraces.

At the Cryptic Oak, her sign opens the rock face, and he creeps in on all fours. As the rock face closes, she slowly elevates herself out of sight until the following evening, when their vivid dancing begins all over again, with wilder than wild fervour.

Their ghostly romps were well known and feared, and people avoided watching them. But one daring man set out to prove he had no fear of the dancing pair. He poked his stick into the earth at the Cryptic Oak and slowly began to feel a slight burning up his arm to his face.

The left side of his face turned red and he developed a burning itch and a rash no one could cure. He had the Devil's Curse, and people avoided getting too close to him. He fled as a stowaway on a vessel, and the alarmed crew threw him overboard and he was drowned.

At the height of shipbuilding in Cardigan, no shipbuilder dared to injure the Cryptic Oak. Anyone who did would pay the price with his own life. The tree was taboo, as many with just one year to live found out. In that year, various accidents and family injuries followed.

One caustic shipbuilder forced one of his workmen to saw off a branch of the Cryptic Oak that he needed to complete his ship. The deed was done in the dark, and later the unfortunate sawyer was found drowned. A hefty section of timber had fallen on him and pinned him into the mud. The incoming tide did the rest.

An eerie brooding fell on the completed ship. On her maiden voyage into the Bay, a sudden leak appeared and the crew took to their dingy.

They watched from a distance in amazement to see the ship right herself and fill her sails. She took a strange course toward Ireland, manned by an invisible crew, and was never seen again.

It was discovered that the shipbuilder who had dared saw off the branch was seen hanging from one of the Cryptic Oak's upper branches. Happy-go-lucky children had robbed the body of any cash, and he was left dancing in the air by his neck, a fitting end.

While he hung above, the Ladi Wen and the Red Devil danced that night, a dance of revenge and ghostly wails of phantom souls in torment echoing across the river. The immortal Ladi Wen and the Red Devil had the night to themselves making whoopee!

Menyw Llwyd
Lady in Grey

On 37 High Street, old Doctor Jones had his surgery. The place was haunted by a white-haired lady who was elegantly dressed in grey. In other rooms of the house, hatmakers were too hard at work to bother with any eerie apparition.

When they saw her walking through the wall, they took no notice, as it happened all the time. Doctor Jones, every inch an elderly gentleman, would lift his hat off as she passed. She never acknowledged his courtesy.

Y Bedd Heb Farw
The Grave That Refused to Die

A young wife suddenly died. For months the raw upturned earth retained its earthiness, and not a single blade of grass grew on it. The flowers left on her mound remained as fresh as the day they were placed there.

Her grief-stricken husband, devastated at his loss, pined himself to his own death. He was buried with her, but then the flowers wilted away, and a rich green carpet soon covered their grave.

Did the ghost tend her own grave while waiting for her husband?

Afterword

This collection of Cardigan ghost tales marks my first attempt to bring my grandmother's and mother's stories together in a single book. They embrace not only my family's existence but also the old fireside tradition of telling little known and forgotten tales.

They are important to me, this local store of uncanny folktales, transmogrifications, and ghost stories. With these stories, will today's Cardigan residents discover a greater pride in their forgotten ancestry and the heritage of their ghostly beginnings?

These fireside tales, whether mystical or mortal, record the fears and uncertainties of their time. They reveal how people's imaginations tried to explain, through beliefs and superstitions, the many things that were beyond their understanding.

The wonders of the mortal Earth and the ever-changing universe, and how we are swayed by their unseen influences: the Sun and the Moon and the vastness of the starry Milky Way, where Gwydion, son of Don, went searching for his erring wife, Welsh ghosts in space. Our hearing is at fault; we are not able to listen to the swirling, echoing toll of the universe at large.

How the old Cardigan moons waned and shivered in silence and solitude! Those silences brooded over my childhood years; we were ignorant and innocent of the natural and unnatural worlds. I (we) grew up in a ghostly atmosphere. In front of the fire we sat with troubled expressions. The flames gave a glint to our eyes, and the creepy tales held our fascination. We loved those spellbinding evenings. Memories of them take me back to spend quiet hours reminiscing; they echo in my mind.

Some evenings are so still, so deathly still, when I have the kitchen to myself. Outside the moon is pushing back the darkness. The clouds go dark, and then there is a sudden bright moonlight. When my family returns, I feel safe and comfortable beside the built-up fire.

Mam Mam Cei's voice touched our hearts. Her dream-world eloquence had matured through sorrowful memories. She was old and the evenings were young, and she spun tales from the old spirit world to a young audience.

She seemed stirred by the incoming tides and the gale-force winds that howled down the chimney. Our humble grandmother seemed forged out of the elements, and we will never hear nor see the likes of her ever again.

Mam Mam Cie, Maria Morgan.